John Bruckner

Criticisms on the Diversions of Purley in a Letter to Horne

Tooke

John Bruckner

Criticisms on the Diversions of Purley in a Letter to Horne Tooke

ISBN/EAN: 9783337109806

Printed in Europe, USA, Canada, Australia, Japan

Cover: Foto ©Thomas Meinert / pixelio.de

More available books at **www.hansebooks.com**

CRITICISMS

ON

The DIVERSIONS of PURLEY, &c.

CRITICISMS

ON

The DIVERSIONS of PURLEY.

IN A

LETTER

TO

HORNE TOOKE, Esq.

BY I. CASSANDER.

NUGAS AGIT, SED QUÆ AD SERIA DUCUNT.
ERASMUS, Ep. Lib. iv. Ep. 7.

ADVERTISEMENT.

THE remarks contained in the following letter were written three years ago, and merely for the infpection of a few friends, who had expreffed a defire of feeing the Author's fentiments concerning the Diverfions of Purley. This work having been adopted fince by many as a proper guide to Englifh literature, it is prefumed, that the remarks upon it by a writer, who aims at nothing but a fair reprefentation of truth, will not be unacceptable to the Publick. It is pity, indeed, that a performance, in other refpects valuable, and well calculated to open the eyes of the learner with regard to falfe fyftems, fhould remain in its prefent ftate, and not be rendered as perfect as the nature of the fubject will permit.

ERRATA.

PAG.	LINE.	FOR,	READ.
10	22	for	for.
13	26	concerns	concern.
30	19	defortoque	deforteque.
31	6	noits	not its.
39	6	onleꝛon	onléꝛan.
48	21	aꝛculan	aꝛcuꞇan.
Ibid.	—	aꝛleaꝛan	aꝛléan.
49	1	uꞇaꝛtéan	uꞇaꝛlean.
51	9	Adeliꞡg	Adelung.
54	12	Light	Liꞇe.
57	22	Butan	Botan.
58	2	Penanee	Penance.
Ibid.	21	haiꞇ	buloe.
59	14 and 17	Butan	Botan.
64	26	engaarn	ongaarn.
70	1	theis	this.
72	15	hꝑyle	hpýle.
74	21	Spik-fpelder	Spik-fpëlder.

A

LETTER, &c.

SIR,

THE theory of language is a career in which, from the time of Ariſtotle down to the preſent, many an adventurer has run himſelf out of breath ; ſpent himſelf with fatigue, without the applauſe, or even the notice, of the ſpectators. You have had better luck. No ſooner have you entered the liſt, but the eyes of all have been fixed upon you ; and great have been the acclamations at the ſkill and vigor with which you have been obſerved to ſet out.

Your remarks on the diſtribution of language and nature of particles, publiſhed ſome years ago in a letter to Mr. Dunning, and lately republiſhed in your Diverſions of Purley, have excited a general curioſity. Your thoughts are ſo new, your manner is ſo

B   ſhort,

fhort, fo bold, fo expeditious, that it is difficult to fay which has occafioned moft furprife.

It muft not be diffembled, however, that in fome of your pages you have betrayed a very ftrong propenfion towards inaccuracy. Unlefs you can get the better of this failing, much of the luftre which awaits your future publication may be obfcured by it.

The purpofe of this letter, Sir, is to put you, if poffible, upon your guard againft it. The few hints you have given us may, when cleared of the rubbifh which furrounds them, produce fome good ; but no defirable effect can refult from them in the ftate they are in at prefent. I fhall make no other apology for the freedom of this addrefs.

Before I enter upon more important matters, I muft not leave unnoticed your title-page and introduction in your laft-mentioned performance.

An elegant and moft amiable writer has the following obfervation on the monuments which are to be feen in Weftminfter Abbey : " And fome of them " are fo modeft, that they deliver what they have to " fay in Greek and Hebrew, and by that means are " not underftood once in a twelve-month *." How far you were influenced by thefe feelings, when to an Englifh performance you prefixed a Greek title, and how far, after having been the miferable victim of two prepofitions and a conjunction †, you are

* Addifon in the Spectator.

† All I have to fay upon this fubject has been among the loofe papers in my clofet, and would probably have remained there twenty years longer, had I not been made the miferable victim of two prepofitions and a conjunction. Div. of Purley, p. 102.

likely

likely to fuffer from an excefs of modefty, I fhall not take upon me to determine : but with regard to title-pages, I muft beg leave to obferve, that they are never fo pleafing as when they are intelligible ; and wonder much how, after having expreffed fo much horror at Mr. Harris's and Lord Monboddo's zoo-phytes *, that is, " words fignificant without any fig-" nification," you could have the courage of placing a brace of thefe monfters † in your work, by way of frontifpiece.

With regard to your introduction, I muft confefs, that though I have met there with a variety of con-verfation, on a variety of very pleafant fubjects, fuch as " Effufion of Blood, Total Difmemberment of the " Empire, Smoak of London, Boots, Picquet," &c. I have not been particularly ftruck with it, except where you introduce one of the champions for into-lerance, delivering the following maxim, " Whatever " is wavering, involved, ambiguous, muft of courfe " be falfe and fraudulent." This piece of fophiftry, originally levelled at the Proteftant churches, you take up eagerly, and fling it with fome violence in the face of the writer of Hermes, calling out to him with an air of triumph, " I have it from good autho-" rity." That this writer deferves to be chaftifed, may be true ; but that it can be effected with a piece

* Mr. Harris afterwards acknowledges that fome of them have a kind of obfcure fignification—and appear in Grammar like zoo-phytes in nature, a kind of middle being of amphibious character," &c. Ibid. p. 155 and 160.

† Επια πτερουτα, or Diverfions of Purley ; neither of which can give the reader the leaft idea of the fubject in queftion.

of

of a broken fyllogifm borrowed from Monf. De
Meaux, is by no means probable : and how you come
to have recourfe to fuch an expedient is wonderful ;
unlefs indeed you were determined not only to
chaftife him, but to make his chaftifement as igno-
minious as poffible. For what can be more degrad-
ing than to be put to a nonplus with fuch arguments?
It is as bad as being brained with a lady's fan *.
Thus much for your title-page and introduction. I
go over to the work itfelf.

As Grammar is one of the firft arts which probably engaged the attention of the curious, does it
not feem extraordinary that the divifion and diftribution of language fhould remain even to this day fo
imperfect as not to anfwer the purpofe for which it
was contrived ? And yet fo it is. Inftead of point-
ing out, in a clear and diftinct manner, the difference
of words, it may be faid, that, in many inftances, it
ferves only to confound them. In vain, to remedy
this defect, have Grammarians added to the number
of their claffes. They have always found fome words
fo refractory as not to be reducible to any pre-efta-
blifhed clafs whatever ; a circumftance which has in-
creafed the labour of the learner, without any additional advantage. I muft therefore do you the juftice
to fay, that fome praife is your due for having taken
this fubject into confideration, and employed fo much

---

* That the conjunction THAT, and the prepofition OF and
CONCERNING, fhould be made the abject inftruments of my civil
extinction, appeared to me to make my exit from civil life as de-
grading as if I had been brained by a lady's fan. Diverf. of Purley, p. 103.

of

of your leifure upon it. The point of view in which
you have placed it is, upon the whole, well-calculated
to bring within the reach of folution fome of the
difficulties with which it is furrounded.

I fpeak with reftriction, becaufe there is a reafon
for it. If in fome inftances you have cleared the
ground, you have added to its embarraffments in
others, by being too forward in conjecture, too hafty
in decifion, too apt to difplace what is right, and to
fubftitute what is not fo in the room of it. You
have not given, in fhort, your fyftem the confiftency
and folidity of which it is fufceptible, and which
you were very able to give it, had you been willing
to beftow a little more thought upon it. Much of
its credit depends upon neat and eafy deductions with
regard to particles; but, more intent upon the number than juftnefs and propriety of them, your deductions are heaped together without the leaft dif-
crimination; and fuffered, for the moft part, to make
their appearance before they are fit to be feen,
" horridulæ & incomptæ," as the Latins term it. I
muft not, however, allow myfelf the liberty of fuch
remarks without proving them to be juft; and this
will be done in the following pages.

In your firft chapter, which treats of the diftribution or divifion of language, you condemn Grammarians, both ancient and modern, for having fuppofed
that the difference of words may be accounted for
merely from the well-known principle, that language was contrived for the purpofe of communicating thought. You fhew the deficiency of this
principle; and, after a few hints on the means of

rendering

rendering it more complete, you ſtrike out a new diviſion of language ; having, as you ſuppoſe, all the advantages of the old one, without any of its defects. The remarks which I have made on this chapter will ſhew the contrary.

Whether words are conſidered as the ſigns of things, or ideas, or operations of the mind ; if it be ſuppoſed, as has been done hitherto, that the ſame word may ſerve to repreſent two different things or ideas ; it is impoſſible that the diviſion ariſing from the above-mentioned principle ſhould anſwer the purpoſe, and for this plain reaſon, becauſe one and the ſame word muſt in that caſe neceſſarily belong to two different claſſes.

Had you been ſo fortunate as to view your ſubject in this light, and in no other, ſome advantage might have been gained. Your chapter on the diviſion and diſtribution of language would have been ſhorter, and, what is of more importance, your new diviſion would have been more complete. For want of having, when you planned it, kept your eye fixed on the above-mentioned circumſtance, you miſſed your aim, as others did before you ; and the very ſame miſtakes and inconveniences, which we have to encounter in the old diviſion, diſtreſs us with additional force in your new one.

You do not indeed ſet out from the principle, that there muſt be as many different ſorts of words as there are different ſorts of things, or ideas, or operations of the mind. But you build on a foundation altogether as looſe and precarious, namely, the uſe or deſtination of words.

The

The first aim of language, you say, *was to communicate our thoughts; the second to do it with dispatch* *. And as this principle is two-fold, it leads you, naturally enough, to suppose two sorts of words in language: 1. Words necessary for the communication of our thoughts; 2. Words necessary for the dispatch of that communication †.

I shall not here oppose your two-fold principle concerning the use of language; I shall only take notice of your inference from it. Because language is destined to communicate thoughts, and to communicate them with dispatch, does it follow that there are two distinct and separate orders of words, the one necessary for communication, the other necessary for the dispatch of that business? By no means. One and the same word may happen to answer equally well both purposes. And upon recollection we shall find this not only possible, but actually taking place with regard to a great number of words in every language. If we set out therefore from your principle, *the destination of words,* in order to establish a proper division of them, it will not discriminate them any more than their relation, either to things, or ideas, or operations of the mind. The same words will frequently partake of two different classes; and the new contrivance will leave them as indistinct and confused as ever.

Experience wonderfully confirms the truth of these remarks. Words are divided by you into, 1. *Words necessary for the communication of thought;* 2. *Words*

* P. 37.   † P. 63.

necessary

neceſſary for the diſpatch of that communication. Theſe are your two grand claſſes ; and, provided they do keep the words ſeparate and diſtinct, ſo that no word deemed neceſſary for communication be deemed alſo neceſſary for the diſpatch of that buſineſs, they may remain as they are. But in your firſt claſs are compriſed the nouns in general * ; and among theſe are the general terms ; and the general terms, from your own †, as well as Mr. Locke's definition, are to all intents and purpoſes abbreviations ; and abbreviations are every one of them neceſſary for the diſpatch of communication.

Again : in your ſecond claſs are compriſed articles, prepoſitions, conjunctions, all parts of ſpeech, in ſhort, which do not come under the denomination either of noun or verb, from which they are diſcriminated by the general title of abbreviations or ſubſtitutes, which you give them. But it is generally believed, and we ſhall have occaſion to prove in the courſe of theſe remarks, that among the various words which conſtitute a language, and which are neceſſary for communication, none poſſeſs this laſtmentioned property in a more ſtriking manner than thoſe which you rank under the title of abbreviations, that is, prepoſitions, conjunctions, articles.

You tell us indeed, and that in more than one

* In Engliſh, and in all other languages, there are only two forts of words which are neceſſary for the communication of thought : and they are, 1, Noun ; 2, Verb. Diverſ. of Purley, p. 65.

† Ibid. p. 39.

inſtance,

inftance, they do not poffefs it * : you go even fo far as to try to juggle us into the belief of this paradox.

In your third chapter you roundly affert, and feem to plume yourfelf on the affertion, that without ufing any other forts of words whatever, and merely by means of the noun and the verb, one can relate or communicate any thing that can be communicated and related by the help of all the others †. And here you challenge us to try the experiment. You are not one of thofe, however, who can withftand the force of truth for ever. Soon after this affertion you make ample amends for the boldnefs of it. You acknowledge the article to be at once an abbreviation, and a word neceffary for communication ‡ ; and

you

---

* I am inclined to allow that rank only (viz. of parts of fpeech) to the neceffary words ; and to include all the others (which are not neceffary to fpeech, but merely fubftitutes of the firft fort) under the title of abbreviations. Diverf. of Purley, p. 65. *And again:* Whereas abbreviations are not neceffary for communication. Ibid. p. 96.

† B. Merely fubftitutes! You do not mean that you can difcourfe as well without as with them ?

H. Not as well. A fledge cannot be drawn along as fmoothly, and eafily, and fwiftly, as a carriage with wheels : but it may be dragged.

B. Do you mean then, that without ufing any other fort of word whatever, and merely by means of the noun and the verb, you can relate or communicate any thing that I can relate or communicate with the help of all the others ?

H. Yes: it is the great proof of all I have advanced ; and upon trial you will find that you may do the fame. Diverf. of Purley, p. 67.

‡ The fate of this very neceffary word has been fingularly hard ;

for

you quote Mr. Locke for the further confirmation of this truth.

Thefe are ugly circumftances attending your new divifion of language; and it were greatly to be wifhed you could think of fomething lefs repugnant to common fenfe than words neceffary, and words not neceffary, for communicàtion. You will fay, indeed, the latter are only fuppofed to be fo for the purpofe of keeping them feparate from the others. But the anfwer is obvious. If we are allowed to make fuppofitions in matters of this nature, why fhould we lay afide the old fyftem? It will do very well. *It is only fuppofing an imaginary operation or two*, as occafion requires.

But this is not all. You compare abbreviations to thofe parts of a carriage which have been contrived for eafe, ornament, and luxury; and reprefent them, notwithftanding, as having no connexion with what

for though, without it, the article, or fome equivalent invention, MEN COULD NOT COMMUNICATE THEIR THOUGHTS AT ALL, &c. Ibid. p. 83 and 96.

You add in a note, " for fome equivalent invention. See the " Perfian and other Eaflern languages, which fupply the place of " our article by termination."—As the generality of your readers are not likely to be benefited by this reference, it being rather out of their reach, I beg leave to propofe another in the room of it. The Dano-Saxon language has the contrivance you here mention, or at leaft fomething like it. Porro ut apud veteres Cimbros, vel Danos Gothos, ex nominibus cum articulo vel pronomine in fine affixo nomina compofita, totidemque nominum compofitorum declinationes quot fimplicium—Sic iftiufmodi nominum et declinationum haud pauca reperiuntur veftigia apud Danos Saxonicos Scriptores. Hickes' Gram. H. S. cap. xx. §. 3.

has

has been contrived for the fake of beauty, or any of the above-mentioned purpofes *. You rank under the title of abbreviations, or fubftitutes of nouns and verbs, all prepofitions and conjunctions whatever, though many of them are either nouns or verbs, *ipfo facto*, and at full length; as, *If, An, And, Not,* &c. And to fum up the whole, you divide your abbreviations into abbreviations in terms, abbreviations in forts of words, abbreviations in conftruction; a manner of dividing by no means logical. *Terms* and *forts of words* are appellations which I conceive to be applicable to all and every one of your abbreviations, and very improper therefore to eftablifh any fpecific differences between them. Whether you were aware of this, and took no pleafure in your new divifion; or whether you really thought it had re-

---

* P. 33. Alluding to abbreviations in language, you fay, " But fhould any one, defirous of underftanding the purpofe and meaning of all the parts of our elegant modern carriages, attempt to explain them upon this one principle alone, that they were neceffary for conveyance only, he would find himfelf woefully puzzled to account for the wheels, the feats, the fprings, the blinds, the glaffes, the lining, &c. not to mention the more ornamental parts of gilding, varnifh, &c.

Notwithftanding this comparifon, you fay, p. 37, " The firft aim of language was to communicate our thoughts; the fecond to do it with difpatch. I mean entirely to difregard whatever alterations or additions have been made for the fake of beauty, or ornament, eafe, gracefulnefs, or pleafure.

As in the foregoing paffage abbreviations are evidently confidered as additions made to language, for the fake of beauty, ornament, eafe, &c. one would naturally conclude, from the claufe in the fecond, that you mean entirely to difregard abbreviations in your work, and yet you make them the principal object of it.

ceived all the finishing in your power; you no sooner have brought it to light, than you take your leave of it, and pass over immediately to another chapter. You suffer it, indeed, to appear a second time (p. 69.), but so different from what it was before, that it ceases, in some measure, to be the same. Abbreviations are there divided in the following manner: 1. *Abbreviations in terms*; 2. *Abbreviations in the manner of signification of words.* As second thoughts are generally the best, I am inclined to give this last division the preference, but unfortunately it comes too late to be of any use. These, as I said before, are ugly circumstances in your new distribution of language. They naturally lead to the mortifying inference, that, whatever be your powers of demolishing and destroying, you do not appear to have those of rebuilding what has been taken down.

Many people have long since suspected, as well as yourself *, metaphysics to be a mere cobweb : I will not say with the poet,

         " Fit for scull,
    " That's empty when the moon is full;"

but so thin, so airy, so flimsy, that a man may see, touch, feel, and handle it for some time, before he well knows which is the right, and which is the wrong side of it. And what you advance with respect to Mr. Locke wonderfully confirms this suspi-

* The very term metaphysic being nonsense, and all the systems of it, and controversies concerning it, that are, or have been, in the world, being founded on the grossest ignorance of words and of the nature of speech. Divers. of Purley, p. 450.

cion :

cion : " *I confider,*" you fay, " *the whole of Mr.
Locke's Effay as a philofophical account of the firft fort
of abbreviations in language ;*" and you add, " *Perhaps it was for mankind a lucky miftake* (FOR IT WAS
A MISTAKE) *which he made when he called his Effay,*
AN ESSAY ON HUMAN UNDERSTANDING *. Again :
*Had he been aware of this, he would not have talked
of a compofition of ideas, but would have feen that it
was merely a contrivance of language, and that the only
compofition was in the terms* †.

It is evident from your words, that, in your opinion, Mr. Locke was no better than in a mift when
he wrote his famous Effay, as he intended one thing,
and did another. Now, though this may gratify
fome, it will not be perhaps fo pleafing to others.

Mr. Locke is ftill a great favourite in our uni-
verfities. I fhould not wonder at hearing fome young
Wrangler, ready primed from thofe quarters, addrefs
you in the following terms :

" Indeed, Sir, it is not Mr. Locke, it is you, that
" are all this while in a mift with regard to abftract
" ideas. We underftand Mr. Locke very well when
" he fays, *General and univerfal belong, not to the real
" exiftence of things, but they are the inventions and the
" creatures of the underftanding, made by it for its own
" ufe, and concerns only figns. Univerfality does not
" belong to things themfelves, which are all particular
" in their exiftence. When therefore we quit particu-
" lars, the generals that reft are only creatures of our
" own making : their general nature being nothing but*

" *the capacity they are put into of signifying or repre-*
" *senting particulars.*"—But we do not understand
" you, when you express yourself on this subject in
" the following manner: *The business of the mind, as*
" *far as concerns language, extends no farther than to*
" *receive impressions, i. e. to have sensations and feel-*
" *ings ; what are called its operations are merely the*
" *operations of language* *. We do not call a con-
" stellation a complex star, nor a pair of bellows
" complex bellows, nor a pound of figs a complex
" fig. But we say *a complex being, a complex name, a*
" *complex sign, because* we conceive the particulars to
" coalesce so as to make but one. Why should we
" not say a *complex idea?* If in the latter case we
" conceive an absurdity, we do no more than you do,
" when you conceive words to be at once absolutely
" necessary and not at all necessary for communica-
" tion †. And now we are upon that chapter, what
" is your principle of dispatch, but a fifth wheel to
" a carriage, more fit to retard than to accelerate its
" motion ? *Language,* say you, *is intended not only*
" *for the communication of thought, but moreover for*
" *the dispatch of that communication.* Upon this sub-
" ject I shall observe,

" 1. That if any circumstance, beside the desire
" of communicating thought, influence the mind in
" the contrivance of language, it must be that of
" communicating, not so much with dispatch, as with
" clearness and precision. When we speak, the first

* P. 70.
† See what has been said above concerning the article, p. 11.

" thing

" thing we aim at is to be underftood, and to raife
" in the mind of others the fame confiderations and
" affections as engage our own. And whatever be the
" particular caft of the fign we ufe, it is the refult
" of that intention. *Men learn names, and ufe them*
" *in talk with others, only that they may be underftood,*
" fays Mr. Locke; and this is likewife the fentiment
" of Mr. De Broffe, which has been quoted from you:
" *On ne parle que pour être entendu ; le plus grand avan-*
" *tage d'une langue c'eft d'être claire.* You fuppofe,
" indeed, that, notwithftanding this formal declara-
" tion, he is well aware of the fitnefs and expedi-
" ency of your fifth wheel; as he fays afterward,
" *L'efprit humain veut aller vite dans fes operations,*
" *plus empreffé de s'exprimer promptement, que curieux*
" *de s'exprimer avec une jufteffe exacte et réfléchie.*
" But this is mere imagination. Monf. De Broffe,
" in this latter paffage, no more thought of your
" abbreviations, than he thought of Alioth in the
" tail of the great bear: he only meant to fay, that
" if men are not always exact and precife in the
" bufinefs of fpeech, it is becaufe they chufe rather
" to have done with it, than to give themfelves any
" trouble about it. I obferve,

" 2. That there are few words in language whofe
" origin, nature, and particular character, may not be
" traced from the above-mentioned principle. You
" yourfelf allow that it accounts for the introduction
" of noun and verb. And as to the reft, nothing
" can be a ftronger indication that they proceed from
" the fame fource, than the particular energy they
" have in producing, with the others, the fame effect.
" Without

" Without them, our meaning is vague and uncer-
" tain * : but no sooner are they brought into play,
than

---

* According to the very learned Schultens, this energy of the
article is no where more confpicuous than in the Oriental languages. Quintilian had advanced, that the Latin language could
do very well without the article. Upon which this author makes
the following remark: " *Cæterum articulum non defiderare Latinum
Sermonem, gloriofius dictum quam verius putem* . . . . *Ne de Græcis
jam loquar, Orientales noftri incredibilem quandam vim orationis cum
elegantiffima brevitate par articulum affecuti.* Inftitut. ad Fundam
Linguæ Heb. §. CIV.

Is it poffible that the *incredibilis vis,* & *elegantiffima brevitas,* here
afcribed to the article, are the refult of a mere defire of difpatch
in the communication of thought ? and fhould we not look out for
fome more regular caufe in the production of this effect ?—I quote
here Profeffor Schultens, becaufe he was an excellent judge in
thofe matters ; and to convince you of it, I fhall adduce but one
proof. Long before you thought of it, that is, about fixty years
ago, he had laid it down as a fact, that " GRAMMARIANS HAD
" ALL ALONG MISTAKEN THE ROAD WHICH LEADS TO THE
" PROPER EXPLANATION AND ETYMOLOGY OF PARTICLES,"
concerning which he expreffes himfelf thus. Inflit. Sectio VI.
§. XCI. in a note.—*Minus commoda* Cl. Altingii *inter particulas de-
clinabiles,* & *indeclinabiles. Ad priores refert pronomina. Ad pofte-
riores, adverbia præpofitiones,* & *conjunctiones.—A'qui* & *pronomina
quædam non declinantur,* & *bona pars adverbiorum ac præpofitionum
patitur declinationem, quippe quæ, maximam partem, fint vel nomina
vel fubftantiva, vel adjectiva. Hoc fi perfpexiffent primi Grammatici,
multo felicius naturam, vim, mutationem,* & *conftructionem particularum
expedire potuiffent,* Again, §. XVI. *Particulas reliquas, fub quibus
adverbia, præpofitiones, conjunctiones,* & *interjectiones comprenfa minus
rite indeclinabiles vocari dictum. Ratio hæc, quod revera declinentur
præfertim adverbia,* & *præpofitiones ; utpote veri nominis, fubftantiva
vel adjectiva, maximam partem. Rectius in feparatas,* & *infepara-
biles dirimuntur. Separatarum claffes diftinctius notabo: atque fub fin-
gulis fpecimina quædam exhibebo :* and immediately after comes a
long

" than it becomes vifible and palpable. But, fay
" you, it cannot be denied, that they wonderfully
" accelerate communication. True. But that pro-
" perty I look upon as an acceffory, not a principal,
" in the ufe for which they were intended. They
" fhorten communication ; becaufe without concife-
" nefs, i. e. reducing the number of terms, there
" can be no communication.

" 3. As the principle of difpatch in communica-
" tion is not neceffary to account for the diftribution
" of language, fo neither for the many difputes and
" errors about this matter among philofophers. They
" wrangled and blundered about it, plainly becaufe
" it never occurred to them that particles were, for
" the moft part, no more than verbs or nouns derived
" from ancient language. This accounts much bet-
" ter for the matter in queftion than any thing elfe
" that can be faid upon it. And fhould you ever
" meet poor Harris in the walks of fome future Lu-
" cian or Fontenelle, it is not improbable he would
" accoft you in the following manner : You were
" very fevere, Sir! in your ftrictures upon my Her-

long ftring of Hebrew adverbs, prepofitions, and conjunctions,
which he proves to be no more than nouns in that language ; and
then finifhes with the following obfervation : Apud Latinos quo-
que conjunctiones multæ a nominibus oriundæ, *Ut verùm, verò,*
verum enimverò, quemadmodum, quamquam, additum & verbum in
quamlibet, quolibet, quovis.

Mr. Schultens adheres to this plan in all his writings. He endeavours every where to banifh from the theory of languages all
notions of myftery, all kinds of anomalies, and to account for the
nature of every part of fpeech, by bringing it as near as poffible to
its firft origin.

C   " mes

" mes when above. What induced me to write that
" book was not the defire of offending you, or any
" perfon whatever. I was actuated by the fame mo-
" tive which urged you to write your Diverfions of
" Purley. I wifhed to difcover what had remained,
" till my time, a fecret among my countrymen. I
" mifcarried; becaufe I faw no trace of noun or
" verb in the words I wifhed to explain. Hence
" my flights in the higher regions of metaphy-
" fics. If I have been too daring, why fhould
" you avail yourfelf of my failure to depreciate my
" talents? Am I then the only one who has pre-
" fumed upon himfelf? and have I dipped my pen in
" gall to hurt the feelings of any one? Health, fpi-
" rits, ingenuity, may carry a man through any
" wicked practice in the world we came from. But
" here, Sir, nothing can fupport us but the remem-
" brance of our good actions; and as this is the mea-
" fure of our happinefs, let us endeavour to make it
" as great as we can by forgetting, I, my Adequates
" Preventives; and you, your Anglo-Saxon Etymo-
" logies."

In this, or fome fuch manner, will the Lockifts
give vent to their rage, when they come to anfwer
your ftrictures on their Mafter's Effay. For my part,
I fhall not undertake to defend the propriety of his
expreffion, with regard to fuch aggregates of ideas
as conftitute the claffes, gender, fpecies, and which
he calls *complex ideas.* I am not fond of labouring
in vain; and it is evident from your difcoveries, that,
in thefe matters, it is the eafieft thing in the world
for a man to do his utmoft, and mifs his aim after all.

1 fhall

I shall only observe, that, as the thing signified must necessarily exist before the sign, there is a striking absurdity in representing the former as a mere effect of the latter: and one is inclined to suspect these to be your notions, when, speaking of abstract ideas, you say, " *it is a mere contrivance of language; the* " *only composition is in the terms, and not in the ideas.*" p. 49. And again, " *The business of the mind, as far* " *as concerns language, extends no farther than to re-* " *ceive impressions; that is, to have sensations and* " *feelings; what is called its operations, are merely* " *the operations of language.*" May it not be inferred from these expressions, that, in your opinion, it is the term that gives birth to the abstract idea, and not the latter to the term? And if you deny it, will not the whole of this laboured dissertation dwindle into a mere logomachy?

As to the circumstances which may have attended the desire of communicating thought, and influenced the nature and order of the signs contrived for that purpose, I will not go so far as to say, with those I have taken the liberty of introducing here, that the desire of dispatch had no share in that contrivance, as it would be an easy matter to prove the contrary. But I must beg leave to observe, that I do not believe it the only, nor even the principal, circumstance to be taken into consideration, in order to account for the division and distribution of language.

The desire which arises in the mind, next to that of communicating thought, is certainly to use such signs as will convey the meaning clearly and precisely; which naturally leads to the use of abbrevi-

ations,

ations, as without them, according to your own ideas, this end cannot be attained. p. 245. Abbreviations, therefore, feem to bear a much ſtronger affinity to the deſire of *perſpicuity* than to that of *diſpatch*. This latter, conſidered by itſelf, feems little calculated for any regular purpoſes. It may produce abbreviations, but of the kind only to which Monſ. Le Préſident De Broſſes alludes, when he ſays, *L'eſprit humain veut aller vite dans ſon opération* ; *plus empreſſé de s'exprimer promptement, que curieux de s'exprimer avec une Juſteſſe réfléchie. S'il n'a pas l'inſtrument qu'il faudroit employer, il ſe ſert de celui qu'il a tout prêt :* When guided by the former, it produces conciſeneſs, but conciſeneſs attended with neatneſs and perſpicuity.

After the deſire of perſpicuity in the communication of thought comes that of variety ; a deſire ſo deeply rooted in human nature, that it looks for the gratification of it in every object it contemplates, in every ſtudy it purſues, in every amuſement it partakes. " *All the ſenſes delight in it, and equally are* " *averſe to ſameneſs,*" ſays an ingenious artiſt. (Hogarth, Analyſis of Beauty, chap. II.). *The ear is as much offended with one continued note, as the eye is with being fixed to a point, or to the view of a dead wall.* Can it be imagined that it had no hand (if I may be allowed the expreſſion) in the contrivance of ſound for the communication of thought ? All our ſenſes lead us to a contrary ſuppoſition : and experience teaches us, that it interfered in the framing of language, even ſo far as to give birth to a ſort of words which otherwiſe would not have appeared in it. For what are pronouns but words of that
kind ?

kind? The principle of difpatch in communication, on which you lay fo much ftrefs to account for the origin and nature of particles, is therefore by no means fufficient for that purpofe. It is the truth, but not the whole truth. It may interfere in the contrivance of the article, conjunctions, and prepofitions; but as a fecondary, not a ruling principle. The only circumftance, in which it acts in the laft-mentioned capacity, is apparently in vulgar elliptical forms of fpeech.

Advertifement, p. 102.

It is generally at the beginning, immediately after the title-page, that this tedious and troublefome part of a book makes its appearance. In yours it does not come forth till about the middle of it; perhaps as good a place as any, efpecially if the author means ferioufly to have it perufed. For, as the French fay, *L'appétit vient en mangeant*, I fhall therefore, without any farther hefitation, follow your example, and add here what I have to fay by way of advertifement.

I. Anglo-Saxon literature is, no doubt, an object worth the attention of the people of this country. In order to underftand the meaning and drift of the excellent laws under which we live, it is neceffary we fhould have fome knowledge of the language of thofe who made them. Your defire, therefore, of promoting the ftudy of it among your readers, and your prefenting them, for that purpofe, with a table of its alphabetical characters, is liberal, and what one might naturally expect from a public-fpirited man as you are. However, as nothing is more likely to prove fatal to that ftudy than unforefeen impediments at the firft

fetting

fetting out, you muſt allow me the liberty to ſay, that your table is not altogether ſo compleat as it ought to be. It wants the wings of Mercury ; the abbreviations, without which there can be no diſpatch in communication. This is the fiſt hint I wiſhed to give you by way of advertiſement.

II. As I am not without fears about your ſucceſs, and expect that the Lockiſts will ſoon appear in a body againſt you, I have been examining your outworks again ; and as I find them abſolutely untenable, I would adviſe you to abandon them in caſe of a regular attack, and to ſhut yourſelf up in your capital work, which is of good deſign and workmanſhip, and will ſtand the beſt battering-ram in the world, provided however you beſtow a little repairing upon it. In what follows, I ſhall point out to you the places where this is moſt wanted ; and begin with the chapter of the nouns, on which I ſhall make two remarks.

Firſt, In matters of little or no conſequence, men in general, and even the wiſeſt, are very prone to take, upon the credit of others, what they will not take the trouble of examining themſelves ; and this moſt likely was the caſe when Dr. Prieſtley aſſerted, upon the credit of Mr. Harris, that *Moon* is of the feminine gender in the Northern languages, as it is in the Greek and Latin. Had Mr. Harris aſſerted likewiſe, that two and two make five, it is more than probable the Doctor would not have taken his word for it. Be that as it may, he was unguarded when he took it for granted that Mr. Harris could not be miſtaken in a point ſo much in his way : but ſo are you (excuſe my freedom) when, writing upon this matter, you boldly

boldly declare, " *that in all the Northern languages of* " *this part of the globe which we inhabit,* MOON *is* " *masculine.*" I do not know the *Icelandic, Lap-landish*, or *Greenlandish*; but I know the Low Dutch tolerably well, and take upon me to say, that *Moon,* ' *Maan*, in that language is feminine; and so feminine, that there is no boor in Holland whose ears would not be shocked at hearing one say, *Het light des maans*, instead of *Het light der maane*, the light of the moon. It is particularly unfortunate for you to have made this stumble at your first onset against Mr. Harris.

It were to be wished (and this is my Second Remark), that you had been a little more explicit upon the reason which you assign for the English language not admitting a gender in the nouns of things inanimate. This, you say, is owing to the circumstance of the relation of nouns being expressed in it by the place or preposition. But is not this the case also in the French, Italian, and Spanish? And yet in every one of these the nouns in question class among those which have a specific gender. The truth is, that, in all other languages (not including, however, those I am not acquainted with, as the Samoyede, Esquimaux, Assinipoul, &c.) the relation of gender is expressed, not, as you suppose, by the place and preposition, but by an inflexion, either in the noun or article prefixed to it. But the noun in English being susceptible of inflexion only in a few instances, and the article in none, it is no wonder that a distinction of the specific gender should not take place in it at all with regard to the nouns in question. But it is

wonderful,

wonderful, that fome * fhould have reprefented it as
an ornament, and the refult of thought and contrivance, when in fact it is a blemifh †, and merely the
effect of chance. Any one converfant with the hif-
tory of the Englifh language, knows that it formerly
admitted that diftinction, as the Dutch and Frific do
to this day; and that it did not lofe this mark of
its defcent till after the Conqueft; when it was fo
much altered by the mixture of the French or
Norman, as to become in fome meafure a new language. We may take it for granted therefore, that
the fame circumftance which caufed Anglo Saxon
nouns to take a French termination for the formation
of the plural, and French verbs Englifh ones for the
diftinction of tenfe, number, and perfon, influenced
likewife the gender of their nouns, and caufed it to
be omitted, and grow at laft obfolete, in thofe that
were appropriated to things inanimate.

* Harris and Lowth. By whom we are given to underftand,
that, for want of this contrivance, no language, except the Englifh,
can keep clear of ambiguity and obfcurity in the Profopopoeïa.
Had it been confiftent with the gravity of their character, they
might have added the following ftory, which would have been
much more to the purpofe. A meffenger was fent to the Queen of
Navarre, with a letter, and ordered, *de la baifer en la lui préfentant:*
and fo the blockhead kiffed the Queen, inftead of the letter; which
could not have happened, had the French language been without
gender for the name of inanimate things.

† It muft be confeffed, that, by affixing a gender to every noun,
the Greek and the Latin will, in many inftances, and more particularly in elliptical forms of fpeech, admit of a concifenefs and
perfpicuity of expreffion, which is peculiar to them, *Calida lavari,
frigidam bibere,* ἰς τὰ μάλακα φορῖντις.

Καλέσι δ᾽ Ἰοκάστην μι᾽ τῦτο γὰρ πατὴρ
ἔθετο·

See Valckenaer in Euripidis Phœn. v. 12.

Interjections

As opprobrious language is not uſual with you, eſpecially when there is no occaſion for it, one is ſurpriſed to hear you rail at the interjections, and call them *brutiſh and inarticulate ſounds, which have nothing to do with ſpeech, and are only the miſerable refuſe of it.* But, when a man has bragged to his neighbours of the ſpaciouſneſs of his houſe, has laid a conſiderable wager, has ſworn a great oath, that it will contain them all ; and finds himſelf, upon trial, more pent than a negro on board an African trader, or a forlorn hope in the houſe of an Amſterdam Zieleverkooper,—what can he do, but turn out ſome, and call them a parcel of low-lived ſcoundrels who intrude themſelves into gentlemens' company ?

As you had aſſerted that there were but two ſorts of words in language, words neceſſary for the communication of thought, and words neceſſary for the diſpatch of that communication, the interjections could not but prove extremely troubleſome. You perceived immediately that they could by no means whatever be forced into either of your claſſes ; and yet they had by preſcription an undoubted right to the place they occupied among the parts of ſpeech. To alter your claſſes, was giving up your words neceſſary for the diſpatch of communication, and that would have been a pity. To meddle with the other claſs, was bringing down the whole edifice at once, and that would have been terrible. No wonder if you fretted and fumed, and came at laſt to the reſolution

lution of ufing, with thefe *foi difants* parts of fpeech, the fame liberty as the Emperor Jofeph ufed with the monks in Flanders—and fo—turned them out. This I take to be the beft reafon which can be given for your violent and arbitrary proceedings againft the poor interjections. And had not fome propitious circumftances intervened, you would very likely have been as cruel to the article.

The general terms being by themfelves indefinite, as to the extent of their fignification, it is evident that fome fign is wanted to fix the fenfe in which they are to be taken. And as this is the office of the articles, it is not lefs evident that they are as neceffary for the communication of thought, as the general terms themfelves can be; and therefore it would be madnefs to refufe them a place among the parts of fpeech. But they are neither nouns nor verbs; nor can they, in the ftrict fenfe of the words, be called abbreviations of them, becaufe they have not a fingle feature belonging to that fpecies. They were therefore in no fmall danger of undergoing the fame fate with the interjections, if by great good luck you had not contrived to difpofe of them, by fuppofing a fecond kind of abbreviations or fubftitutes, befides thofe you had already contrived. The firft were abbreviations or fubftitutes of known words in a language; whereas the fecond kind, which was to comprehend the article, is abbreviations or fubftitutes of words not known in language.

" *From the neceffity of general terms* (I quote your
" words) *follows immediately the neceffity of the arti-*
" *cle, whofe bufinefs it is to reduce their generality,*
" *and*

" *and upon occafion to employ general terms for parti-*
" *cular; fo that the article in combination with the*
" *general terms is merely a fubftitute. But then it dif-*
" *fers from thofe fubftitutes which we have ranked*
" *under the general head of abbreviations, becaufe it is*
" *neceffary for the communication of thought, and fup-*
" *plies the place of words not in the language; whereas*
" *abbreviations are not neceffary for communication,*
" *and fupply the place of words which are in the lan-*
" *guage *.*" The beginning of this period is unex-
ceptionable; but the latter part of it is by no means
fo.

Subftitutes of words which are not in language. As
thefe words muft needs form a very numerous tribe,
it is wonderful, fome will fay, how you could fo
eafily find out fuch as were more particularly in want
of fubftitutes. I defpife fuch remarkers, fay you.
" *Thefe are the people who have the accent neither of*
" *Chriftian, Pagan, or man; nor can fpeak fo many*
" *words together with as much propriety as Balaam's*
" *afs did †.*" Hold, Sir!—thefe are alfo the people
of whom it has been faid, with no lefs propriety,
C'eft une nation puiffante, Dieu en a béni la race ‡ !
You will do better, therefore, to keep upon good
terms with them; and the more, as in the prefent inftance you have no manner of advantage over them.

There is reafon to rejeᵉt, in a great meafure, your
notion of the article. It is a fubftitute, no doubt;
but if there be cafes in which it is evidently the fubftitute of words which are in the language, why

---

* P. 96.   † P. 43. in a note.   ‡ La Fontaine.

ftould

fhould we go upon an idle chafe, and hunt for words not in the language? Numberlefs are the inftances in which it anfwers this purpofe in the Greek, and in fo pointed a manner, that it is hardly poffible to miftake the words for which it ftands. I fhall quote a few; and if you wifh for more, you may fee a cloud of them in Vigerus's Idiotifms *.

It ftands for ὕος in the following phrafe, ἄγεσθαι τὴν ἔπι θανάτῳ ad mortem rapi—for ἡμέρα, in—τῇ προτεραία, i. e. pridie—for ἀπόφθεγμα—in—τὸ τῇ Σολῶνος for ὑιος in ὁ τῇ Δεμοσθένης. And if I were to affirm, that, in Englifh, French, or Flemifh, there is not an inftance in which the definite article does not ftand for the name of the gender, fpecies, or difference of the thing in queftion, I believe I fhould not go beyond the truth. And I adhere to this hypothefis the more firmly, as, without it, it is hardly poffible to account for the article being placed in thefe languages fo frequently before particular nouns. Before the general term it may be faid to reftrain, or rather determine, the fenfe in which that term is to be taken, and more efpecially in the French. But what fhall we fay, when it is placed before a particular name, as in thefe inftances—*the fun*—*the moon*—*the earth*—*the fky*—*the clouds?* There is no reduction nor reftriction whatever in any of thefe cafes; yet the neceffity of the article is marked in them as ftrongly as any where. Its deftination, therefore, is not confined to the ufe you mention; it evidently anfwers fome further purpofe.

* Cap. III. Sect. 1. Reg. 3.

The

The human mind is for ever bufy in treafuring up every thing which comes within the reach of its perceptions; and, that its ftores may be of ufe and always at hand, they are divided into various claffes; and every clafs has its peculiar name : by which means every perception becomes at once diftinct and communicable. By calling over the claffes, we find a name for any object whatever ; and at the fame time that we retain fome idea of it ourfelves, we can, when we pleafe, make it known to others. In either cafe, the name of the clafs is always the firft thing which obtrudes itfelf upon the mind ; and that name is moftly underftood in the article which immediately precedes the particular name of the thing in queftion.

Sun, Moon, Stars, belong to that clafs of beings which are called the heavenly bodies ; and it is that clafs I mean to exprefs when I fay, The Sun, The Moon, The Stars. This becomes unqueftionable from the following inftances. *The Mediterranean* is evidently the Mediterranean Sea ; *The Pyrenees*, the Pyrenean Mountains ; *The Bermudas*, the Ifles fo called. Again, *the wall, the garden, the yard*, manifeftly indicate a whole, of which thefe are the particulars ; and the name of that whole is expreffed, or at leaft indicated, by the article prefixed to the name of the particular. The French ufe it before the names of countries : they fay, *La France, L'Italie, L'Efpagne* ; becaufe thefe countries are by them confidered in thefe expreffions as parts of a whole ; and that whole is Europe. They alfo fay, *L'Europe, L'Afie, L'Afrique* ; and then that whole is the habitable earth. In fhort, there is hardly an inftance

in thofe languages, in which the reference of the
article (which is called the definite) to words known
in the language is not palpable *. Your placing it
therefore

* For the further elucidation of this matter, I beg leave to quote
here a few remarks which I made fome time ago on the ufe of the
article in the French language.

L'article étant deftiné à marquer les différens fens dans lefquels
fe peuvent prendre les noms appellatifs & communs ; il femble
qu'il devienne, en quelque façon, inutile avant les noms, qui ne
pouvant défigner qu'un objet à la fois, font par cela même incapables
de varier, pour ce qui regarde l'étendue de leur fignification. Ce-
pendant il n'eft pas rare de voir ces noms précédés de l'article.
On dit, par exemple, *L'Etienne qui a écrit l'Apologie pour Hérodote.
Le Clodius qui fe déchaina contre Cicéron. On trouve dans l'hiftoire
des Juifs un Zaccharie, tué dans le temple avant la venue du Meffie.*
C'eft que dans ces façons de parler, on confidère l'individu portant
tel ou tel nom, comme appartenant à tel ou à tel ordre de perfonnes,
dont le terme commun eft d'être toutes appellées de même. De-
fortoque le nom propre devient ici un nom appellatif, & comme
il fe prend dans un fens particulier, il faut néceffairement, qu'il foit
précédé de l'article défini.

Mais il y a des noms propres qu'on donne à des êtres, en quelque façon uniques, & qui font néamoins précédés de l'article.
Ainfi, quoiqu'il n'y ait, fuivant la façon de penfer des hommes en
général, qu'un feul foleil, qu'une feule lune, qu'une feule terre, on
dit malgré cela avec l'article, *le foleil, la lune, la terre.* Parceque
chacun de ces êtres tient à un tout que l'on a toujours préfent à
l'efprit quand on les veut nommer, & auquel on les renvoye vifi-
blement, en mettant l'article avant les noms qui les défignent.
Quand on dit *L'Europe* ou *L'Afie,* on fent que cette idée en réveille
d'abord une autre qui lui fert, pour ainfi dire, de bafe ; & cette
idée c'eft la terre en général, que l'on fait être divifée en certaines
portions, & qui fe préfente comme telle à l'efprit, dès qu'on entend
nommer quelqu'une de ces portions. Or c'eft pour faire fentir le
raport à l'idée qui lui fert de bafe, et en même tems pour la diftin-

guer

therefore in the oppofite light, in order to diftinguifh it from thofe fubftitutes which you call fubftitutes of words known in the language, is prepofterous and unfatisfactory. For though we fhould allow it to have the ufe here affigned to it (which we do not allow at prefent), yet, as it is no its general character, it is wrong to build upon that, and that only, its fpecific difference, from fubftitutes of words known in the language. As to the latter, we have feen already with what propriety they are ftiled, without any exception, *fubftitutes*; when moft, if not all of them, are in fact the very words of which they are fuppofed to fupply the place. Nor fhall I repeat here what I have faid concerning your hypothefis, of their not being neceffary for communication. I have made it appear pretty plain, that you had yourfelf no great confidence in it.

guer des autres portions, qu'on fe fert de l'article avant le nom qui lui eft propre.

En général on peut dire, que l'article avant les noms des êtres que nous avons nommés uniques femble les défigner, ou comme parties d'un tout, ou comme individus de quelque efpéce; & dans ce dernier cas, l'article tient lieu en quelque façon du nom appellatif; ou ce qui revient au même du nom de l'efpéce. Ainfi *La Baltique*, c'eft fans contredit, *La Mer Baltique*; *La Seine*, la riviére de la Seine; *Le Véfuve*, le mont appellé Véfuve. Manière de s'enoncer parfaitement analogue à célle dont on conçoit ces chofes, & que l'on retient encore toutes les fois que les noms des individus font trop vagues pour en donner des idées bien diftinctes. Ainfi on dit *Le fleuve St. Laurent*, *Le lac Champlain*, *Les Ifles Philippines*.

Chapter VI. Of the Word THAT.

Except what relates to politics, which, though ever so found, cannot with any propriety be introduced into a work of this kind, the whole of this chapter deferves attention. The light in which it reprefents the ftructure of language is curious; and if you go on folving in fo plaufible a manner this intricate bufinefs, you will make ample amends for the little recreation we have met with hitherto in the Diverfions of Purley.

I beg leave, however, to make a few remarks on the word THAT.

There are inftances in which it does not feem fufceptible of the fenfe into which you refolve it: fuch are thofe where it is connected, in one and the fame phrafe, with the pronoun perfonal IT; as for inftance, *It is reafonable that we fhould do by others, as we would be done by ourfelves*; *It is not to be expected that in a ftate of tryal like the prefent, we fhould meet with no difficulties*; *Be it known, that*, &c. Again, when it is preceded immediately by the word *intent* in the dative cafe, as, *To the intent, that when they come up, they might teach their children the fame.*

It feems as if in the preceding inftances the word THAT could not admit of your refolution, without introducing both redundancy and coufufion. Whatever, fay you, be the name which is given to it, whatever be its fituation and appearance, it is one and the fame word, namely, the article, and ftands for THAT THING. But is not the fenfe of this laft expreffion
implied

implied already in the pronoun IT, which begins the two firſt of the preceding phraſes? And if ſo, is there not a kind of awkwardneſs and redundancy in the article which follows? It is very poſſible, however, that it will admit of your reſolution, without my being aware of it. I am far, therefore, from alledging theſe inſtances as proofs that you are wrong. I give them only as difficulties which may be thrown in your way. And of the ſame nature is the next remark.

In the dead languages, the ſenſe of the words which conſtitute a phraſe depends on their termination chiefly; whereas, in the modern languages, this point is principally determined by their reſpective poſition. There is but one poſition, either in Engliſh, French, or Dutch, which can be given to the words expreſſing the ſenſe of the following Latin phraſe, *Petrus amat Deum :* the leaſt alteration in it will affect its meaning, and make it either nonſenſe, or at leaſt the reverſe of the ſenſe which is intended. Each word, therefore, in the modern languages, has its particular poſition, from which it never departs, except for the ſake of the metre in poetry. And this poſition depends entirely upon the ſpecific difference of words.

Whether our forefathers had, or had not, ſigns by which to expreſs this difference, they certainly were ſenſible of it; as no word, in their language, any more than in ours, ever took the place of another, but all had their fixed and peculiar ſtation, according as they were either nouns or verbs, &c. As this is a

D

well-

well-known truth, I ſhall adduce no proof for the
confirmation of it, but paſs on to its application.

Is it not remarkable, that the word here in queſtion
ſhould occupy different places in the Anglo-Saxon *,
and in its kindred the Dutch, the Friſic, the German,
according as it ſtands for a pronoun, or a conjunction; that in the former inſtance it ſhould be
placed between the auxiliary and the participle, and
in the latter after the participle in the compound
tenſes; that as a pronoun governed by the verb,
it is placed thus, Ic hæbbe ðæꞇ ꞃæƀe; and when
uſed as a conjunction in this manner, ic hæbbe
ꞃæƀe ðæꞇ?—But this is not the only inſtance in
which it aſſumes a different turn according to the
different purpoſes for which it is uſed. When in
the ſhape of a pronoun, it has no kind of influence
over the words which follow: whereas it makes a
total change in their order if it ſtand for a conjunction. So if, in tranſlating the following phraſe, *I tell
thee now Siward* THAT *I have here already ſet down
theſe few briefes of ancient bookes*, you make *That*
a pronoun, the ſentence will be in the Anglo-Saxon
as follows: ic ꞃecꞅe þe nu Ziꝼeꞃð ðæꞇ, ic hæbbe
heꞃe ꞅeꞃecðaꞅ ꞃeaþa býꞃna oꝼ ðan ealban bocum:
but if you make it what is commonly called a con-

---

* To thoſe who attend only to the rules of poſition in the Engliſh, the Anglo-Saxon language may ſeem uncouth and uncon-
nected, as it did to Dr. Johnſon; but that it is ſo in fact, no one
acquainted with the rules of poſition, either in the German or
Dutch, will affirm. Theſe rules form a very important object in
the ſtudy of thoſe languages, and will apply to the Anglo-Saxon
in every particular.

junction,

junction, the next arrangement will take place, ꞇ ꞃecꞅe þe nu Zꞇꞃepþ ᵭæꞇ ꞇ hep ᵹeꞃeꞇꞇ hæbbe, &c.*

The fame holds with regard to the Dutch : your firſt example, *I wiſh you to believe*, &c. tranſlated in that language, will have, if you ſuppofe THAT a pronoun, this appearance, *Ick verzoek u te gelooven dat* (ding) *Ick bezeer niet gaarn eene vlieg*. If a conjunction, the following, *Ick verzoeke u te gelooven dat ick niet gaarn eene vlieg bezeere*. Here you fee the verb finiſhes the ſecond part of the ſentence ; whereas, before, it begins it. But enough of THAT.

Conjunctions in your fyſtem, are not indeclinable or feparate parts of ſpeech having a certain manner of fignification by themfelves, but words belonging to the fpecies either of nouns or verbs, and which by a ſkilful herald may be eaſily traced home to their own family and origin. As the origin of the word IF, fo eaſily difcoverable, is extremely favourable to this way of thinking, it is with great propricty you begin with it your etymological conjectures.

IF is certainly the imperative mood of the Anglo-Saxon verb Gꞇꝼan ; for in this language, as ſtill in the German and Dutch, the imperative mood is formed by dropping the termination of the infinitive mood AN or EN. The imperative mood of the Anglo-Saxon verb Gꞇꝼan can be no other therefore than Gꞇꝼ. And this is the very form in which the conjunction IF makes its appearance in old Engliſh authors, as you have fufficiently proved. It is made, indeed, to govern the fubjunctive mood; an influence,

---

* Ancient Monuments in the Saxon Tongue, by M. L'iſle, Lond. 1638.

fome

fome will fay, which could hardly be afcribed to it, were it confidered merely as an appendix to the verb Gıɲan. But it is not improbable that this circumftance, together with many others, in the modern languages, is owing to the exceffive care of fome dunces, who having been whipped feverely, when young, for neglecting the proper government of conjunctions in the Latin, have contracted the habit of making their equivalents govern with them the fame mood in other languages. Now for An, from the verb Anan, to give.

I have known a public fpeaker who would now and then take a furvey of his audience, and call out (if he efpied any drooping noddles or falling jaws) " Brethren, I will tell you a ftory." As I think this an excellent method of roufing the attention of a reader or hearer, for ever inclined to grow drowfy when the fubject is fo, I fhall not fcruple to make ufe of it upon this occafion.

It is well known that the boors in Friefland, one of the United Provinces, have fo far retained ancient cuftoms, as to be, in drefs, language, and manners, exactly the fame people which they were five hundred years ago ; a circumftance that induced Junius the fon to pay them a vifit, and to pafs a few months among them. In a tour I made to that country fome years ago, I was at a gentleman's houfe, from which I made frequent excurfions into the inner part of the Province. In one of thefe, I was obliged to take the firft fheltering place in my way, being overtaken by a violent fhower. It was a farm houfe, where I faw feveral children : and I fhall never forget the

fpeech

fpeech which one of them, an overgrown babe, made to his mother. He was ftanding at her breaft; and, after he had done with one, I heard him fay to her, *Trientjen yan my 't oor*; i. e. " Kate! give me " t'other." I little thought, at the time, I fhould have fo good an opportunity of making ufe of this ftory as I have at prefent.

AN, you fay, is the imperative of the verb ANAN, juft as IF is the imperative of GIFan. I confefs this latter deduction is fo plain, fo natural, and fo fatis-factory, that it affords great encouragement to take it as a model for all the reft. But we fhould not fancy that words exift, or muft have exifted, becaufe, having adopted a certain method of finding out ori-gins, we cannot poffibly do without them. I have been looking out with fome anxiety for the Anglo-Saxon verb ANAN, but can get very little informa-tion about it. I find, indeed, in King Alfred's will the following article : Æpyꞇ ic an Eaꝺpaꝺe minum elꝺpa puna. *Firſt, I give to Edward my eldeſt ſon.* And from the expreffion IC AN, it fhould feem as if there really exifted fuch verb in the Anglo-Saxon as ANAN. But as this is the only fign of life it has given, as one may fay, for thefe thoufand years, I am inclined to look upon that fign as being rather equi-vocal, and fufpect that the true reading of the will is, not ic an, but ic un, from unnan *cedere, concedere*; this laft verb being common in the Anglo-Saxon, and nothing more eafy than to miftake an u for an a, in that language, as well as in the Englifh. How-ever, as I have not feen hitherto any manufcript, on whofe authority I can ground the juftnefs of my

con-

conjecture, I do not give it you as any thing certain; and if you perfist in giving the preference to the old reading, the ftory of the babe is certainly in your favour; for there is as little difference between An and ẏan, as between Un and an. With me it will remain a matter of doubt, whether there ever exifled fuch a verb as Anan, the fame in fignification, and yet different in origin, with Gɪꞃan. It is by no means probable, that a people, who had hardly a conveyance for one idea in a thoufand, fhould have procured two fuch noble conveyances for one fingle idea. This is a piece of luxury, which even the moft civilized nation feldom allow themfelves.

The next word you undertake to explain according to your principles, is UNLESS. You fuppofe it to be the imperative of the Anglo-Saxon verb un-leꞃan, to difmifs. But to thofe who, like me, judge from analogy, the propriety of this derivation is by no means obvious. *We cannot love God, difmifs he prepareth our hearts. No man cometh to my father, difmifs my father draweth him. Difmifs you repent, you fhall all likewife perifh.* The turn which language has taken with regard to this expreffion will not bear fuch phrafeology. The *Latin*, the *Italian*, the *French*, make ufe here of the word *except.* The *Anglo-Saxon* and the *Dutch* of its equivalent, ucneman uẏtneemen ...... which feems more natural, and which muft have had the preference from time immemorial: fince, according to the paffage you very properly quote from *Feflus*, even the ancient Romans ufed it inftead of NISI. For *Nemut* is a word fo like the imperative mode of *uẏtncemen,*

2   both

both in found and fenfe, that there is great reafon to
believe that it is an adoption from the Teutonic verb. ·
But this is not the only reafon I can alledge againft
your hypothefis; it is not even the ftrongeft.

If there be fuch a verb in the Anglo-Saxon, it
muft be the fame with onleyon, a compound of on
and leyan, and the Dutch *ontloſſen:* but neither leyan
in the Anglo-Saxon, nor LOSSEN in the Dutch, fig-
niñes *to difmiſs.* Leyan, in its primary fignification,
means to *unbind;* in its fecondary, to *redeem,* to *un-
load, to fet at liberty. Solvere, redimere, liberare,* fays
the dictionary. In the firft fenfe it anfwers to the
Englifh, *to loofen,* i. e. *to make loofe;* in the fecond,
the Dutch *ontloſſen.* Skinner, indeed, tranflates on-
leyan, or rather aleyan, *to difmiſs.* But Skinner is
often ignorant, fays Dr. Johnfon * ; and I reject his
tranflation, becaufe I am certain the equivalent in
Dutch *ontloſſen* is not fufceptible of it.—But further.

As there is an equivalent in the French of the
word UNLESS very much refembling it in turn, it is
fomewhat extraordinary, that it fhould never have
occurred to you, that poffibly the one is a tranflation,
or at leaft an imitation of the other. This equivalent is A MOINS QUE. What word more likely to
have given birth to *unleſs;* if we may fuppofe the
latter to be a compound of *on* and *leſs?* And if the
Anglo-Saxon dialect admits of *onlaſt,* at the laft ; *onbæc,*
at the back ; *onbutan,* externally ; *on æffe,* oppofite ;
why fhould it not alfo admit of *onleſs,* for A MOINS
QUE ? This conjecture is the more probable, as it

* Preface to his Dictionary.

was

was not till after the Conqueft, when the Englifh became a mixture of the French and Anglo-Saxon, that the word UNLESS was introduced into it; the Anglo-Saxon having ufed till then, as you yourfelf have obferved, NEMTHE, or NYMTHE, inftead of it. And yet you never mention A MOINS QUE; no, not even where you name the words correfponding in other languages to the Englifh word UNLESS. The French SINON, unlefs you add QUE to it, which you do not, is by no means of the number. It is fometimes ufed as an adverb in the fenfe of *otherwife*, or *in default*. *Faites ce qu'il dit, finon, n'efperez nulle grace de fa part*; *do what he bids you, elfe expect no favour from him*. Sometimes as, *venia fit verbo*, an exceptive conjunction, when it muft be tranflated *but*. *Je n'ai autre chofe a vous dire, finon que vous en uferez comme il vous plaira*; *I have nothing to tell you, but that you are at liberty to do what you pleafe.* p. 214.

LES. *The imperative of* Leran.

The orthography of this word, I prefume to fay, is LESS. It is thus Ben Jonfon fpells it in the paffages you here quote from him; and it fhould feem as if civilized people had no other way of fpelling it. You choofe, however, upon the authority of Gawin Douglas, to write it with a fingle s; and, truly, I do not wonder at it, as in that garb it will anfwer your purpofe much better than in the common one. It is poffible that LES fhould be the imperative of Leran; but LESS can have no pretenfions to it: at leaft not according to your principles; for, if my

memory

memory does not deceive me, you have faid fomewhere, or at leaſt given us to underſtand, that words
may loſe, but not acquire, letters, as they recede
from their origin.

You do not depend, however, in ſo implicit a
manner upon Gawin Douglas's ſkill of ſpelling, as
to adopt it upon every occaſion. You ſcruple not
to depart from it wherever it proves unfavourable to
ſome new etymology. A ſtrong proof that the mo-
tive I have juſt now mentioned has no ſmall degree
of influence over your judgement in theſe matters.
No ſooner has the imperative of the Anglo-Saxon
verb Leꝼan ſhewn itſelf with you in one form, than
it appears in another. In the very next article to
that we are upon here, you ſuppoſe it to be, not LES,
but LEAS: and why ? becauſe you labour to prove
there that *Leafleas, Botleas,* and the like Anglo-Saxon
words, are compounds of a noun and the imperative
in queſtion, which would not have been quite ſo
clear, had that imperative appeared in its uſual
form. But, it will be ſaid, how can Leaꝼ be the imperative of Leꝼan ? Verbs may loſe, but not acquire, letters, as they recede from their origin.
Whether you were aware of this difficulty, and
wiſhed to make yourſelf eaſy about it, or whether
chance ſo far interpoſed in your favour as to remove
it without your knowledge, I cannot tell. Certain
it is, that the verb Leꝼan is here all of a ſudden
transformed into Leoꝼan ; in conſequence of which,
its alliance with the affix Leaꝼ becomes unqueſtion-
able. But Leoꝼan ſignifies *perdere,* and is the ſame
verb with the Engliſh to *Loſe*...... Oh, we cannot
hel⸗

help that, you'll fay. We have proved Leaʃ to be the imperative of it, and that's fufficient.

You add in a note *, It is the fame imperative Les, placed at the end of nouns, and coalefcing with them, which has given to our language fuch adjectives as HOPELESS, RESTLESS, DEATHLESS, MOTIONLESS. Thefe words have been all along confidered as compounds of *Hope, Reſt*, &c. and the adjective *Leſs*, Anglo-Saxon Leaʃ †, and Dutch Loos : and this explanation is fo natural, fo clear and fatisfactory, that it is inconceivable how a man, who has any notion of neatnefs and confiſtency in etymological difquiſitions, could ever think of their being compounds of a noun, and the imperative of the verb Leʃan. LEAS and Loos are ſtill extant, this in the Dutch, and that in the Anglo-Saxon language ; and both anſwer to the Latin *folutus* in this phrafe *folutus cura.* So that *bopeleſs*, in the literal fenfe of the word, only means *void of hope* ; *faithleſs, void of faith* ; a fenfe fo obvious, and fo analogous to that which we mean to exprefs when we ufe thefe words, that nothing but love of novelty in the extreme could induce you to reject it, in order to make room for the uncouth and awkward expreſſions, *Hope-diſmiſs, Death-diſmiſs*

---

* P. 126.

† Multa (adjectiva) formantur ex fubſtantivis addendo affixum negativum Leaʃ, vel Léaʃe, ut pecceleaʃ *negligens* ; ʃcommeleaʃ, *impuncus*; ezeleaʃ, *impavidus* ; ʃacleaʃ *fine culpa.* Hinc apud nos *careleſſe, fatherleſſe, motherleſſe, friendleſſe, harmleſſe,* & fimilia. Sciendum vero cſt leaʃ Anglo-Saxonicum deduci a M. Gothico Lans, quod fignificat *liber, folutus, vacuus,* & in compofitione privationem vel defectum denotat. Hickes's Angl. Sax. Gram. IV. §. III.

Where, in the name of wonder, have you ever found words tacked together in this manner?

In all languages, as far as we know, which admit of compofition in words, there is a certain manner which muft be attended to, before we prefume to make compounds; a manner in the arrangement; and a manner in the choice of thofe words which are to be joined together. Some are to be confidered as prefixes, others as affixes; fome will not coalefce; fome, on the contrary, run into compofition, as it were, of themfelves. In this part of the ftructure, therefore, as well as in all the others, there is a kind of harmony, which muft be attended to, and ferve as a rule. To take words at random, and to jumble them together,

ut nec pes, nec caput,

Uni reddatur formæ,

is to violate that harmony: and this you do, when you tack an imperative to a noun for the purpofe of making but one word of the two. This is a barbarifm of the firft magnitude, I will not fay in the Greek or Latin, but even in the lefs polifhed languages. The French and the Englifh have, indeed, their compounds of imperative and noun, but never of noun and imperative. I mean, that, when fuch compofition takes place with them, the imperative is conftantly placed before the noun *. But, fuppofing

---

* *Un coupe-jarret*, a banditto; *un-boute-feu*, an incendiary; *un tire-bouchon*, a cork-fcrew. So in Englifh, *a cut-purfe, a catch-penny*, &c. We fay, indeed, *a tooth-pick*; but this is evidently corrupt from *tooth-picker*.

it

it was not, neither the French nor the modern Englifh are, in that refpect, a proper ftandard whereby
we can determine the genius of the old language.
Not the French, becaufe it has little or no affinity
with it; nor the Englifh, becaufe it leaves here its
original and more forcible manner, to adopt that of
her rival. The Dutch, as it has preferved to this
day the Anglo-Saxon manner of compofition, and
admits of no other whatever, is undeniably the better
rule to follow on this occafion. But there are no
compounds of the French kind juft mentioned to be
met with in that language : and as to thofe you here
obtrude on your readers, nothing can be more repugnant to its true nature and genius ; a ftrong reafon to believe that they are not admiffible in the
Anglo-Saxon ; and indeed, if they were, the compofition would not have been confined to one fingle inftance. More verbs than one would have had their
imperatives affixed to nouns, in order to make compounds with them. You would not have failed to
quote a few inftances where this kind of compofition
takes place ; and we fhould have had fomething
more than your bare word, by which to regulate our
belief in this particular.

I have not done yet with *hope difmifs* and *faith-
lifmifs* ; I beg leave to add one objection more to
that manner of compofition in language. If, as you
contend, *Loos* be the imperative of *Loffen* in Dutch,
how comes the noun prefixed to the imperative to
terminate with an E, which is the conftant and invariable fign of the ablative cafe ? They write and
pronounce, *vrugteloos*, fruitlefs ; *godeloos*, impious ;
finneloos,

finneloos, fenfelefs ; *lufteloos*, liftlefs. If *Loos* were an active verb, they would write and pronounce *vrugt-loos*, *godloos*, *finloos*, *luftloos*, which is the form of the accufative.

As it is expected you fhould advance fomething in defence of your new-fangled compounds, you make two efforts for that purpofe, but both fo feeble and ill-directed, that neither of them makes the leaft impreffion.

With this view you fay, *I think, however, there will be little doubt about this derivation, when it is obferved, that we fay indifferently either fleeplefs or without fleep*, &c. i. e. *Difmifs fleep*, or *Be out fleep*. *So for thofe words where we have not by habit made the coalefcence, as the Danifh Folkelös and Halelös, we fay in Englifh, without people, without tail*.

We fay indifferently either *fleeplefs* or *without fleep*. Ergo, there can be little doubt of LESS being the imperative of the verb Lefan, &c. Can there be any thing more prepofterous than the ftrefs you lay upon fuch arguments? and who but a man infatuated with the love of fingularity would produce them?

You add, *it is obfervable, that*, IN ALL NORTHERN LANGUAGES, *the termination of this adjective in each language varies juft as the correfpondent verb, whofe imperative it is, varies in that language.*—After which comes an exhibition of the verb Leoran in no lefs than fix different languages*. But here again you

fuffer

---

* As this exhibition is rather curious, I fhall fubmit it to the infpection of the reader.

ſuffer yourſelf to be carried away by your favourite ſyſtem, ſo far as to venture upon ground where you can do nothing but expoſe your want of ſkill. I do not know the Swediſh, nor the Daniſh, nor the Gothic. But I know enough of the Dutch to affirm, without fear of being miſtaken, that the imperative of the verb LOSSEN is Loss, and not Loos, as you put it. Nor can you plead here the negligence of the printer, as no other imperative ſuited your purpoſe ſo well as Loos. And as I find you ſo often and ſo egregiouſly tripping in one of the ſix languages you here appeal to, how can I depend upon what you affirm of the others?

I cannot help taking notice here of the very extra-ordinary ſentence you have been pleaſed to paſs upon Johnſon's Dictionary; a work which, now for many years, has been a kind of ſtandard, by which even the moſt judicious, have aſcertained the ſignification of words in the Engliſh language, and which therefore ought not to be depreciated, without giving weighty reaſons for ſo doing. It has, no doubt, its blemiſhes: but they are not of the kind, *quas incuria fudit.* On the contrary, they may be called the reſult of the oppo-

	Termination.	Infinite of the verb.
Goth	ΛΛΝS	ΛΛΝSϛΛΝ.
Anglo Saxon .	Leaꞃ	Leoꞃan.
Dutch	Loos	Loſſen.
German . . .	Los	Löſen.
Daniſh . . .	Lös	Löſer.
Swediſh . . .	Lós	Löſ.

Div. of Purley, p. 218.

N. B. It is in this table the Anglo-Saxon verb Leꞃan, *ſolvere,* is transformed into Leoꞃan, which has been noticed before.

ſite

fite caufe, too much nicety and exactnefs. Had the author been lefs minute in diftinguifhing the various fignifications of words, he would have faved himfelf a great deal of trouble, and his work would not have been the worfe for it. As it is, we have nothing better of the kind. The explanations are commonly juft and clear; the quotations numerous, and from the beft authorities : which inclines me to believe, that when you ftigmatize it *as a moft contemptible performance, a reproach to the Englifh nation, one third of it being as much the language of the Hottentots as of the Englifh*; you mean only to animadvert on fuch of the Doctor's definitions, divifions, and derivations, as do not perfectly coincide with your manner of difpatching that bufinefs. I am the more willing to make this fuppofition, as you do not enter into particulars ; and as there is perhaps no point in which the Doctor differs more effentially from you, than in the etymologies to be affigned to Englifh particles.

Your mentioning the Hottentots, in a paffage I have juft quoted from you, puts me in mind of your very curious table of Anglo-Saxon verbs * ; one third of which, if I may be allowed the expreffion, are of your own hatching, and fome of them fo cruelly mangled in the hatching, that they have not a limb left entire and in its place.

Beon-utan! Fypᵹan-utan! Mercy upon you for having found fo much fault with others!

Non Di, non homines, non conceffere columnæ !

Why man, there is not a greater adulterator of lan-

* P. 185.

guages than you in the world; and never did Mr. Champante, the Amſterdam ſealing-wax maker in London, violate in a more flagitious manner the purity of the Belgic Dame in his Dutch mottos *, than you that of the Anglo-Saxon in your table.

'. Utan, according to the common way of thinking, is put down in the dictionaries as being both an adverb and a prepoſition; but, whatever you pleaſe to make of it, in neither of theſe capacities can it be joined to the verb in the manner you have done, without violating the moſt obvious rules for the arrangement of words in the Anglo-Saxon langnage; not as an adverb, becauſe, though a word of this denomination is added to a verb in order to expreſs the circumſtance of the matter in queſtion, yet it cannot coaleſce ſo as to make a compound word with it; nor as a prepoſition, becauſe, when this part of ſpeech is to make a compound with a verb, though in other moods it is occaſionally made to follow, yet, in the infinitive, it is conſtantly made to precede it †, and to write anyban-utan, aſculan-utan, aſleaſan-utan,

---

* *Wel brand en vaſt houd.*

† In the German, Dutch, and Anglo-Saxon, the rule is this: in compounds of verb and prepoſition, the prepoſition is always prefixed to the verb in the infinitive, as in unleſan, *ſolvere,* Foſtreaban *conculeare,* Inlaban *introducere:* but, in other moods, ſome of the prepoſitions may be put after it; and this is the caſe, for inſtance, with the prepoſitions up and ute.

Infinir.	Prat.	Imperat.
Upſtanban	ic upſtob, or Stob up	Stanb up
Utſittan	ic utſæt, or ic Sæt ute	Sitt ute.

For want of having attended to this rule, the Editors of Lye's Dictionary

utan, inſtead of utanýðan, utaꝛcutan, utaꝛtean, is as
bad as to write in Latin *Pellere-cx,* inſtead of *Ex-
pellere.*

But I go farther: I doubt whether the Anglo-
Saxon verb Weoꞃðan be ſuſceptible of the compound form you here give it, and I have two
reaſons for my doubts; 1. I am certain the Dutch
Worden is not; 2. .Both in this language and in
the Anglo-Saxon it anſwers to the Latin Fieri;
to the French Devenir, and to the Engliſh to
become, to happen. It is joined to paſſive particles to expreſs the paſſive voice; but ſo as to repreſent, at leaſt in the preſent and imperfeẛ, what is,
or what was doing, and not what is, or was done.
Ƿeoꞃþað beꞃeoꞃðe oꞃ ælcꞃe aꞃe. *Privabantur
omni dignitate.* Ðaꞇ hi anꞃeꞇe ꞃeoꞃðan, Ᵹ Goðeꞃ
ꞃiꝣꞇ luꝼian. *Ut concordes fiant & Dei juſtitiam
ament.*

Similar to Ƿeoꞃðan-uꞇan, and Beon-uꞇan, is
Anan-að in your table: a verb not likely to make

Dictionary have thought themſelves authoriſed to put the prepoſition laſt in the infinitive mood of ſuch verbs as they have found
occaſionally ſeparated from it, when the mood will admit of that
arrangement, and have by that means made, as it were, a ſeparate
order of verbs of them. So in the prepoſition uꞇ, they put
aðꞃiꝼan uꞇ, Ƒuꞃꞃan uꞇ, oꝼꝛlean uꞇ, an arrangement which cauſes
one and the ſame verb, in more than one inſtance, to appear twice,
i. e. once in the article of the prepoſition, and again in that of
the verb itſelf; which is the caſe, for inſtance, in the verbs uꞇa-
ðꞃiꝼan and uꞇlæꞇan. However, when they allow themſelves that
liberty, they keep the verb and prepoſition ſeparate. The fancy
of joining them together, ſo that the prepoſition comes laſt, and
makes, notwithſtanding, a compound with the verb, is entirely
the Author's.

its way in the world, as it confifts of fuch heteroge-
neous parts as never were put together, and labours
under many more unfavourable circumftances. The
conjunction AND is, you fay, the imperative of Anan-
aб, and confequently its literal meaning is, *Da con-*
geriem. I wifh to tranflate *Da congeriem* into Englifh, or French, or Dutch; but whether from flow-
nefs of apprehenfion, or from a real impoffibility,
in none of thefe languages can I find an expreffion
adequate to the purpofe. And how *Da congeriem*
can ever be accoutred with the wings of Mercury,
fo as to pafs currently for one of your ἔπεα πτεροέντα,
or winged words, is to me incomprehenfible. Leaving
you, therefore, to manage that bufinefs, I fhall only
obferve, that, in my opinion, AND is the imperative
of the Dano-Saxon, or rather Franco-theotifc verb,
Andan Spirare, from *Anda Spiritus*; and means fimply
Draw your breath; that is, *Stop, paufe a moment, Sir.*
And fhould you afk, from whence I have my intelli-
gence concerning the verb Anбan, my anfwer will
be, from the fame quarter which furnifhed you with
Anan-aб, *dare congeriem* *. I now proceed to

EKE, where I fhall have occafion to notice another
kind of miftake, into which you are very apt to fall.

---

* The fact is, that we know very little of the origin of AND:
it lies moft likely buried in the ruins of fome ancient language, of
which we do not know fo much as the name. The learned Hickes
fays, that " AND, in the Franco-theotifc, *Ande, Endi, Inte, Int,*
" *Unde, Und,* is a prepofition among the Goths, anfwering to the
" Latin *In, Coram, Contra, Adverfus:* and that fo it comes to be a
" prefix to fo many nouns and verbs in the Anglo-Saxon to make
" with them a compound." Gram. Anglo-Sax. Cap. xiv. §. 37.
This is the whole that can be faid with any certainty of AND.

You obferve, that the conjunction in Dutch is Ook, from the verb Ooken; and in German Auch, from the verb Auchen. I have converfed frequently in Dutch—I have read many Dutch authors—but neither in books nor converfation do I remember ever to have met with this verb Ooken; nor is it to be found either in Sewel's or Halma's Dictionary. With regard to the German Auchen, all I can fay is, that it is not to be found in the Dictionaries I have confulted, among which is Adeling's Wörter-buch, allowed to be the beft of all. You have here, however, the authority of Junius, who puts down thefe verbs as being the origin, the one of *Auch*, the other of *Ook*: but, I have your's to fay, that he was fometimes very carelefs and ignorant; and to add the following moral reflexion, which I find ready cut and dried in one of your pages : *How eafily do men take upon truft, how willingly are they fatisfied with, and how confidently do they repeat after others, falfe expla-nations of what they do not underftand!*

I fee we have not done yet with the imperative of the verb Alefan. Else ; formerly written Alles, Alys, Alyse, Elles, Ellus, Ellis, Ells, Els, and now Else, is no other, in your opinion, than the imperative *Ales* or *Alys*, of *Alefan* or *Alyfan* di-mittere. As my tafte for the Anglo-Saxon has never induced me to attend to the various fpellings of one and the fame word in the language, I fhould think myfelf ridiculous were I to contradict you with regard to the various ways of writing the word Else. I fhall only remark, that had your quotations (by which you mean, I fuppofe, to prove the truth of what you

advance)

advance) been in favour of *Alys*, or *Alyse*, inftead of *Alles*, they would have been more to the purpofe, as the two former come nearer to the imperative in queftion than the latter.

This miftake, however, can make no great differ-ence with regard to the fum total of the credit you are likely to gain by this new difcovery. It is evi-dent, that all thefe different readings of the word Else are refolvable into one and the fame found, viz. that which is expreffed by ELLES. And as this is the form in which the Anglo-Saxon word for ELSE makes its appearance generally, I fhall take it for granted that it is the original one, and with the more confidence, as it has been given to it by Skinner, Minfhew, and Johnfon. Thefe authors agree in de-riving it from the Greek ἄλλως, or the Latin ALIAS : perhaps they are miftaken in doing fo. There is, indeed, as much reafon to fuppofe that the Greeks and Latins borrowed the word from the Germans, as that thefe borrowed it from them ; but that they had it in common will hardly be contefted by thofe who attend a moment to the fimilarity of the found and the fenfe in each of thefe languages ; and confider, at the fame time, the number of words, both in the Greek and the Latin, avowedly of German extraction, or at leaft of the fame origin with their collaterals in the German language.

You will fay that, notwithftanding what has been alledged, your hypothefis is ftill as good as that of Skinner and Minfhew, as both are grounded on con-jecture only. But I cannot allow the derivation of ELSE from, or its alliance at leaft with, the Greek

2   and

and Latin correfponding words to be a mere conjecture, as it is fupported by fact. Æl or El, in
the fenfe of ἄλλως, or *alias*, is ftill extant in the
Anglo-Saxon language; and there are traces of it
not lefs evident in the Dutch and Danifh. The firft
part of this affertion is grounded on the following
words, Ælcoþ, *alias* Ælþeoð, or Æl-þeoðiᵹ, *alienus
peregrinus*, to be found in any Anglo-Saxon Dictionary. The fecond in the Dutch word ELDERS,
and the Danifh ELLERS, fignifying, both of them,
Elfewhere. In both EL feems the radical word, and
ERS only a termination, perhaps that of the genitive
cafe, in order to exprefs a circumftance of time,
place, or manner. AL and EL may then be faid to
convey the fame idea as the Greek ἄλλως, and the
Latin *Aliàs*; and if fo, why fhould we have recourfe
to the verb aleᵹan to find their origin? I have already obferved, that it is not fufceptible of the fignification you have all along affixed to it as its primary one; but let us fuppofe it to fignify *to difmifs*,
and nothing befides; we fhall find many phrafes in
which ELSE will hardly bear to be refolved into *hoc
difmiffo*; witnefs the following, *Nothing Elfe*, *how
Elfe*, *what Elfe*, *where Elfe*.

That, THOUGH, in the Englifh, Ðeah, in the Anglo Saxon, and DOCH, in the Dutch, are one and the
fame word, fignifying one and the fame thing; and
that there is fuch a verb as Ðaᵹian, or Ðaᵹiᵹan, in
the ancient language, is unqueftionable. But that
the firft mentioned words are the imperative of the
verb Ðaᵹian, or Ðaᵹiᵹan, is not quite fo clear.
THOUGH, indeed, is pronounced by fome THAF,

THAUF,

THAUF, or THOF, and by others THO'. But if we
fuppofe (and it is very natural, and even neceffary,
to fuppofe it) that THOUGH had originally a guttural
found at the end (as it ftill has in the Dutch, and
probably in the Danifh), the above-mentioned pronunciation may be accounted for from other circumftances befides that which you imagine. It is well
known, that in words which have gutturals, and are
common to the Englifh and Dutch language, that
found is either dropped in the Englifh, or changed
into that of F: thus, *Nacht* and *Light* are pronounced *Nite, Light*; and *Genoeg, Kuch Sacht,
Enouf, Couf, Soft,* in Englifh. This true and fair reprefentation of the matter, if it do not abfolutely fu-
perfede your derivation of *Though,* renders it at leaft
very uncertain. But I have fomething befides to
alledge againft it.

The true Anglo Saxon word for THOUGH is Ðeah.
For what reafon this word is kept out of fight by
you, I do not know: it is certain, however, that if
it be an imperative, it is not that of the verb Ðaꝼian,
or Ðaꝼiᵹan, which is Ðiꝼ, or Ðaꝼiᵹ. You would
perfuade us, indeed, that this is the form THOUGH
ftill affumes in the provincial pronunciation of it;
but we have feen what dependence can be had upon
this affertion. As Ðeah cannot be called the imperative of Ðaꝼian; fo neither can *Doch,* in Dutch,
pafs for the imperative *Doogen,* or *Gedoogen,* in that
language. As well might one fay, that FED in Englifh is the imperative of *Feed; Rat* of *Rate; Bit* of
Bite. Not to mention, that it is frequently added to
imperatives, to urge in a particular manner the thing

in

in queſtion. As, *Laat toch, toe, Suffer me,* or *Per-mit me, I befeech you.* In which cafe, *toch* feparates the verb from its affix, which it could not do, if it were an imperative.

In your next article * you reprefent *Bot* and *But* as having been originally, that is, in the Anglo-Saxon, two words very different in origin, as well as fignification. Would you be fo obliging, Sir, as to let us know, in what Anglo-Saxon author one is likely to fee this nice diftinction obferved, fo as to be convinced of its reality? You quote, indeed, Chaucer and Gawin Douglas; and, left the quality fhould be contefted, you endeavour to make it up in quantity, having adduced no lefs than twenty paffages from the latter, who, it fhould feem, favours your opinion, and has given you a handle to palm it upon others. But on what ground can he be called, I will not fay, an original, but an Anglo-Saxon writer? I ap-prehend, that neither he, nor Chaucer who lived an hundred years before him, will pafs for one of the number among thofe who ·confider how much the language had been vitiated at the time they lived, by the importation of foreign words †. Skinner taxes the laft-mentioned of the two to have imported whole cart-loads of them; you will give me leave, there-fore, to fufpend my judgement on this your obfer-vation, till you can produce fome better authority for it.

I have my doubts alfo with regard to the origin

* P. 232.   † See Johnfon's Preface, Art. Chaucer.

you

you affign to *Bot*, fuppofing it to be a word really. exifting in the language.

The imperative mood, indeed, has ever been a great favourite with human nature, at leaft fo far as it has the difpofal of it. From the monarch to the mule-driver; from the burgomafter to the mafter of the treckfchuyt; or, if you do not like profane examples, from the dean to the verger, men are fond of it; and there is no doubt, but, as foon as they were able to ufe moods in any way, this was the firft they put in practice. No wonder, therefore, if fome who are wifhing for reputation in the etymological career, but apt to grafp at the laurel before it.is within their reach, fhould, when they meet with words of an obfcure and dubious caft, exclaim without hefitation, " An Imperative! An Imperative!" Aye, aye, men had never any objection to imperatives for their own ufe.

No wonder alfo, if you who have undertaken to explain the moft difficult part of the language, fhould indulge in the fame fancy, and call out upon every occafion, " An Imperative; no other than an Impe-" rative!" But what furprizes me, is the readinefs with which you find at once both an infinitive to your imperatives, and a fenfe to your infinitives, which fuits to a hair the purpofe in queftion.

But, you fay, *is corruptly put for* Bot; *and the latter is the imperative of Botan;* i. e. *to fuperadd, to fubftitute, to atone for, to compenfate with, to make amends with, to add fomething more in order to make up a deficiency in fomething elfe* *. And you add in a

* P. 244 and 250.

note,

note, *Johnson and others have mistaken the expression,* TO BOOT, *(which still remains in our language) for a substantive, which is indeed the infinitive of the same verb, of which the conjunction is the imperative; as the Dutch also still retain* BOETEN *in their language with the same meaning.* The compofure with which you advance your paradoxes, is, indeed, admirable.

As I cannot boaft of having read all the Anglo-Saxon books and manufcripts to be found on this our hemifphere, it would be improper to tell you that I never met the Anglo-Saxon verb BOTAN ufed in the fenfe you are pleafed to give it, viz. TO SUPERADD, TO SUBSTITUTE: I fhall only obferve, that it is not to be found, at leaft not in the fenfe here in queftion, in Somner's or Lye's Dictionaries, or Benfon's Treafure; and as you appeal to the verb BOETEN in Dutch, and mention it as having the fame meaning which you fuppofe BOTAN to have, I muft beg leave to add, that the Dutch verb fignifies *to make amends, to fatisfy, to atone for,* and never *to fupcradd.* Dr. Johnfon has alfo ventured to give us his fentiments with regard to the Anglo-Saxon verb Butan * ; and, more cautious than you are in general, he has confirmed it with proper authority. The fol'owing are his words: BOTAN, *to repent, to compenfate:* as,

He is wis that bit and bote,
And bet biforen dome.

If he be right (and there is great reafon to believe he is) BOTAN in the Anglo-Saxon is exactly the fame verb, in point of fignification, as the Dutch BOETEN.

* See his Dictionary in the word TO BOOT.

To this laſt verb is allied the noun BOETE, PE-NANEE, PENALTY, FINE, ſays Sewell; and to the Anglo-Saxon BOTAN is allied BOT, *recompenſe*, ſays Johnſon very properly, *or fine paid by way of expia-tion.* BOETE and BOT may very ſafely, therefore, be taken for the ſame word. To BOTE in the Anglo-Saxon is applied properly to what is paid or done by way of making amends for an offence; and thence, in a ſecondary ſignification, to what is paid or done in addition to the value offered or received between two contracting parties: in which ſenſe it anſwers to the common expreſſion in Engliſh, *into the bargain*; and to the French, *Par deſſus le marché.* And as theſe expreſſions may be extended, in both languages, to whatever exceeds, either in ſpeaking or acting, the object firſt in view; ſo the Anglo-Saxon TO BOTE takes a greater or a leſs latitude of ſignification, as occaſion requires. I ſhall give, for example, a paſſage borrowed from Somner, and tranſlated for the purpoſe into Engliſh and French.

Ang. Sax. Oꝼte he to bote halbe ᵹecpeðon þ hie ðeꞃ piᵹeꞃ piᵹh te ne pohton.

Lat. *Sæpe inſuper ei audacter dixerunt, ſe victorem nibili facere.*

Eng. *They told him into the bargain, more than once, and boldly, that they regarded not the conqueror.*

French. *Ils lui dirent par deſſus le marché, & cela avec hardieſſe & à différentes repriſes qu'ils n'avoient pour le vainqueur que du mépris.*

I uſe here the words *into the bargain*, and *par deſ-ſus le marché*, not becauſe I think them elegant ex-preſſions, but becauſe they are the beſt to render the

ſenſe

enfe of the Anglo-Saxon word *to bote*; and prove
evidently that words may, in a remote fignification,
convey an idea no ways connected with the primary
fignification of the root from which they fpring.

If any one were to tell you that BARGAIN in Englifh,
MARCHE, in French, and INSUPER in the Latin, in
confequence of the meaning they here affume, are all
defcended from verbs, the primary fignification of
which is to SUPERADD, or SUBSTITUTE, would you
not think this a ftrange way of reafoning? Now I
am defirous to know what ground you have to go
upon with regard to the fignification of the Anglo-
Saxon verb BOTAN. It can be no other than this:
To BOTE, if not the verb BUTAN itfelf, is nearly related to it. To BOTE, Anglo-Saxon, is the fame
word as TO BOOT in Englifh, and fignifies *infuper*;
ergo, *Butan* fignifies to SUPERADD, or SUBSTITUTE!
Armed with fome fuch argument, it is pleafant to
hear you pafs the following fentence. *Johnfon and
others have miftaken the expreffion* TO BOOT *for a fubftantive, which is indeed the infinitive of the fame verb
of which the conjunction is the imperative.* Permit me
to fay, there is not the leaft ground for this ftricture.
BOOT is evidently the fame word with the Dutch
BOETE, and differs from it in the fpelling only.
BOETE, to my certain knowledge, is not a verb,
but a fubftantive. To BOTE, Anglo Saxon, moreover, cannot be an infinitive; becaufe no words com-
ing under that denomination are likely any more in
the Anglo-Saxon than in the Dutch to end in OTE,
or any termination exhibiting a confonant between
two vowels; but it may be a fubftantive; and that it
actually

actually belongs to this clafs is evident, from the in-flexion it undergoes in confequence of the prepofition being prefixed to it. This inflexion is the E at the end of it, the invariable mark in the Anglo-Saxon of an oblique cafe in nouns of that caft. All nouns mafculine in that language, ending their nominative with a confonant, take E in the dative or ablative: GOD, GODE; ENGEL, ENGELE; GROUND, GROUNDE. Ða cpæð Zacchapiaſ to þam enȝele, &c. Ða anþ-ſapoþe him ſe enȝel. Ic eaom Ðabſiel ıc ſtanþe beſoſan Ðobe *.

I could quote more paffages to prove my affertion; but as it is hardly poffible to add any without being tirefome, I fhall be permitted, I fuppofe, to come to the following inference.

There is great reafon to believe that Johnfon and others have not miftaken the expreffion TO BOOT, when they called it a fubftantive; but that you were egregioufly fo, when you made an infinitive of it.

I am now come to the word BUT, in the fenfe of WITHOUT, or the Latin NISI. You give it as your opinion, that it is a contraction of the Anglo-Saxon BUTE, or BUTAN, and anfwers to the Dutch BUYTEN; and thus far I perfectly agree with you: but when you add BUTE, or BUTAN, is neither more nor lefs than BE OUT, i. e. an imperative of the verb ute-beon, I beg leave to confider a moment.

Se that hinne felve uorget.

. . . .

He fal comen on cucle ftede
But Gode him be milde.

* See Specimen of Ancient Englifh in Johnfon's Preface.

He

He who forgets himſelf ſhall come to an evil fate,
Be out the Lord be merciful unto him.

    There nis met bote frute
    There nis halle bure no bench.
    Bot water man is thurſt to quench.

There is no meat, be out fruit; no hall, no houſe, no bench : nothing be out water for a man his thirſt to quench.

As an imperative implies a command, and this a ſubjeƈt to whom it is given, the perſon who ſays, *Be out fruit, be out water,* muſt be ſuppoſed to give his orders to ſomebody. Now, unleſs we admit he is here addreſſing his own words, I confeſs I cannot ſee the ſubjeƈt to whom his ſpeech is direƈted. We ſay indeed, *Be it known, be it remembered*; but then, *to you,* or *by you,* is underſtood. We ſay, *If you come,* i. e. *give you come*; but there again the ſubjeƈt is viſible; however, let us not be too nice, we often hear of a man eating his words : why ſhould we not believe that a man can addreſs his words ? the one is not more impoſſible than the other. If there be any real objeƈtion againſt your explanation of BUTE or BUTAN, it muſt be the following.

Numberleſs are the inſtances in which Be is employed as a prefix; and in others as a prepoſition in the ſenſe of CIRCA *juxta, per, in, ſecundum,* in the Anglo-Saxon, Dutch, or Engliſh. And unleſs we can aſſign a ſignification to it, which will make it one and the ſame word, whatever be its appearance, it matters not to name one which will ſuit only in this or that inſtance. For you ſay very properly, " *I do* " *not allow that any words change their nature, ſo as to* " *belong*

" *belong fometimes to one part of fpeech, and fometimes*
" *to another, from the different ways of ufing them.*"
Whatever, therefore, be that in which the word in
queſtion is uſed, it muſt have one and the ſame form
as well as meaning, when traced to its ſource. But
if we look over the catalogue of words in an Engliſh
or Dutch dictionary beginning with it, we ſhall
hardly find one in twenty, nay, in an hundred, which
will bear the ſuppoſition that its firſt component part
is neither more nor leſs than the imperative BE, from
the verb To BE.

The field of conjecture is open to all; and whatever riches are diſcovered in it, they are the property of the diſcoverer, and he may reap the benefit
of them without fear of ever becoming an object of
cenſure or envy, provided he does not preſume to
circulate them as ſterling. To indulge in fancies
where we have little or no ground to go upon, is a
harmleſs amuſement; but to proffer the reſult of our
ſpeculations under thoſe circumſtances, as any thing
which can be depended upon, is prepoſterous.

So many ages have elapſed ſince the Anglo-Saxon
language firſt began to be diſtinguiſhed from any
other, it continued for ſo long a ſpace of time to
float in the mouths of ſavages and unſettled people,
it underwent ſo many changes from the mixture of
foreign idioms, that probably the rudiments from
which it ſprang are for the moſt part loſt: and without theſe, it is impoſſible to trace the origin of every
word that occurs in the language. It is but now and
then we ſee a ray breaking through the clouds which
obſcure

obſcure this ſcene ; but now and then we can make
an obſervation.

We ſee enough, however, to fix our judgement
with regard to the true nature of prepoſitions, conjunctions, and particles in general : ſome of them
have ſo near a reſemblance to words conſidered as different from them, and ſtill remaining in the language,
that it is more than probable both belonged formerly
to one and the ſame claſs.—Ἀλλα, for inſtance, in
the Greek language, called a conjunction, can be nothing but the noun ἄλλα, πράγματα being underſtood—Ergo, in the Latin, the dative or ablative
caſe of the Greek noun ἔργον *—On, in the French,
the Italian noun *huom, or uom* †—Not in Engliſh,
and Niet in Dutch, compounds, the one of ne and
ought, and the other of ne and iet : this laſt word
having the ſame ſignification as ought in Engliſh.

I mention this explanation of the word Not, becauſe it appears to be more natural and ſatisfactory
than that which you have given of it, p. 512, of your
Diverſions of Purley ; where, after ſome ſtrictures on
Greenwood's, Minſhew's, and Junius's derivation, you
expreſs yourſelf on this ſubject in the following
manner : *But we need not be any further inquiſitive,*

* See Sanctii Minerva de Vocibus Homonymis. L. IV.

† Il peccato per lo quale huom dice ch'io debbo, eſſera morte
giudicato, io no'l commiſi giammai.　　　　　Bocace.

Il ſonno veramente è com' uom dice,
Parente della morte.

Petrarque.

ner,

nor, I think, doubtful, about the origin and fignification of NOT *and* NO, *fince we find that in the Danifh* Nödig, *and in the Swedifh* Nödig, *and in the Dutch* Noode, Node, *and* No, *mean averfe, unwilling.*

Nothing can equal the inadvertence, to fay no more, which you betray upon this occafion. Had you beftowed one fingle thought upon the fubject, you would not have put down No as a Dutch word ; nor would you have called Noode or Node an adjective equivalent to Nödig in the Danifh, and Nödig in the Swedifh, and having with them the fignification of AVERSE, UNWILLING.

Noode, in Dutch, is the dative or ablative cafe of Nood, neceffity ; and is an abbreviation of Uyt noode, *through neceffity.* What is done through neceffity, may be faid to be done unwillingly and with averfion. Thefe different expreffions, therefore, are put down in the dictionaries as being equivalent, and the following phrafe, *Dat heb ick noode gedaan,* may be found there tranflated, *I have done that unwillingly.* But does it follow that Noode is an adjective fignify-ing *unwilling, averfe ?* As well might a Dutchman fay that NECESSITY, in Englifh, is a word of this clafs, having that fignification, becaufe *I have done it through neceffity* ; is thus explained in his dictionary, I have done it, unwilling, or averfe, *Iik heb het en-gaarn gedaan.*

From the fimilarity of the found and fpelling, I fhould fufpect *Nödig* in the Danifh, and *Nodig* in the Swedifh, to be the fame word with *Nodig* in Dutch ; and, if fo, its proper and primary fignifica-tion is *Neceffary,* and not that which you are pleafed

to

to affign to it, *Unwilling, Averfe*. And from this, and many other circumftances, I fufpect, moreover, that your knowledge of the Swedifh and Danifh is of the fame kind with that you poffefs of the Dutch—the mere refult of fome occafional infpection into the dictionary. Be that as it may, your derivation of Nor is abfurd beyond meafure ; but, abfurd as it is, you make it your finifhing ftroke. It is after this fpecimen of your etymological powers, you tell your reader, as if confcious of fomething, I do not know what, *I hope I fhall be permitted to have done with etymology* ; and fo——you take your leave of him.

Without, *nothing but the imperative of* Ɣyпꝺ-uꝼan. To many this derivation may appear plaufible; but not fo to thofe who underftand any thing of the Dutch or the German : they will tell you, that Ɣeoп-ꝺan will not coalefce with the prepofition ut or utan, fo as to make a compound word with it, any more than ex with fieri in Latin ; out with *become* in Englifh ; and *hors* with *devenir* in French : they will tell you, moreover, that very different are the verbs Beon and Weordan ; . and that if, by faying the one is incorporated into the other, you mean that both have the fame fignification, you are utterly miftaken. But no more at prefent of Weordan-utan : it ought never to make its appearance but to be laughed at.

You accufe Hermes of having blinded philofophy ; take care you do not commit a greater crime, poffeffed as you are with the rage of ftuffing the language with words repugnant to its nature ; take care you do not poifon the hallowed fprings at which the Englifh Mufe delights to drink : the limpid ftream may

foon

foon lofe its purity, if the courfe of it be altered.
You tell us, that thofe who have no coaches muft ride
in fledges : but in your way there is no riding at all,
not even upon a ftick ; and if the rude forefather of
the hamlet had no other way of communicating
thought than that you mention, he muft have felt
happy whenever he could keep his thoughts to himfelf, as by that means he efcaped a hooting.

1. Afs be out a crupper.
2. Man join a nofe.
3. Figs come beginning Turkey.

This is the way in which he expreffed himfelf when,
in the firft inftance, he wifhed to fay, *An afs without
a crupper* ; in the fecond, *A man with a nofe* ; in the
third, *Figs come from Turkey* *. It is very well he is
gone ; had he lived to the prefent wicked age, he
muft have had a bad time of it.

* FROM, *you* fay, p. 374, *means merely* BEGINNING, *and nothing
elfe* ; *and immediately aft r you add*, it is fimply the Anglo-Saxon or
Gothic word FRUM, *beginning, origin, fource, fountain, author*.
Ergo, fome will fay, it means fomething more than *beginning*. But
I will not dwell upon this inference. There certainly is fuch a
word as *Frum, Frim*, or *Fram*, in the ancient language ; and among
the fignificaticns affixed to it by Lye, is that you mention ;
but by the uncouth, unmeaning interpofition of it in *Figs come
beginning Turkey*, one would naturally imagine, that either the
primary fignification of it is loft, or that the expreffion is elliptical,
and wants fome intermediate word or words to fill up the chafm. It
feems, indeed, a difficult matter to fay any thing rational concerning the particular drift, rot only of this, but of many more words
without having recourfe to one of thefe fuppofitions. *Frym* and
From are very likely allied to *Form, Forma*. *Primus*, and it is not
improbable, that both are cerved from the word *For*, originally a
noun ; but what the original meaning of that word is cannot be
afcertained.

Junius,

Junius, Skinner, Wallis, Johnson, and Lowth, all concur in deriving LEST (a conjunction) from LEAST (adjective). You are very positive it is not derived from it: "*I will venture to affirm*, say you, *that* LEST, "*for* LESED, *is nothing else than the imperative of* "LESAN *dimittere*; *and, with the article* THAT, *either* "*expreffed, or underflood, means no more than hoc* "*dimiffo*, or *quo dimiffo*."

And I also will venture to affirm fomething, which is, that there is great reafon to reject, on this occafion, if not your hypothefis, at leaft the confidence with which it is delivered; and if my affertion prove true, *it will furnifh one caution more to learned critics*, (I give your own words), *not to innovate rafhly: left, while they attempt to amend a language, as they imagine, in one trifling refpect, they mar it in another of more importance; and, by their corrupt alterations and amendments, confirm errors, and make truth more difficult to be difcovered by thofe who come after them.*

BETAAL * is a very common word among the Dutch; it is generally the firft one one hears when one lands any where in their country; and truly the Englifh are not much behind hand with them in the ufe of its equivalent. For fince they obferved, that by urging it frequently their neighbours grew fat and lufty, and fufficiently ftrong to meddle with other people's things without afking leave, they alfo became fond of it; and the imperative LES, from the verb LEZAN, was no more common among the Anglo-Saxons, than the imperative mood of the verb to PAY is among your modern Englifh: they ufe it even

* The imperative of BETAALEN, to pay.

in

in contracts of mutual civility, infomuch, that when, on the one fide, is to be given up a certain portion of judgement and belief, and, on the other, certain good reafons for it, they will not give you a pennyworth of the firft article, unlefs you *pay* them ten times the value.

In the name of wonder, will you fay, what do you mean by this ftrange digreffion? It is intended, Sir, as a hint that your countrymen will not pin their faith upon your affertions, and pay you a compliment into the bargain, unlefs you fhew caufe why they fhould do fo.

On what ground does your etymology of the particle here in queftion reft, that you fhould be fo pofitive about it? Lest for Lesed, fay you, as Blest for Blessed. This is the whole of what you tender for our deference to your opinion; and, fmall as the confideration is, it is made up of bad coin.

Lesan and Blessian cannot, whatever you may think of the matter, be coupled together, as belonging to one and the fame order of verbs; the one has a fingle, the other a double confonant before the termination of the infinitive mood: that forms a long, this a fhort fyllable in the participle paffive; and confequently, though the latter will bear the contraction, it does not follow that the former will bear it likewife. And thus much for the bad coin with which you attempt to put us off.

Chillingworth fays, no matter where, *You make ufe of fuch indirect and crooked arts as thefe to blaft my reputation, and to poffefs mens minds with difaffection to my perfon, left peradventure they might, with fome in-*

difference,

difference, hear reason from me. And the following is the turn you give this paffage, in order to fhew the juftnefs and efficacy of *hoc dimiffo.*

" *You make ufe of thefe arts.*" Why ? the reafon follows, *Lefed that,* i. e. *Hoc dimiffo—Men might hear reafon from me—Therefore you ufe thefe arts.*

Would any one imagine this curious aphorifm to be intended as an explanation of the particle LEST, to fhew at once, and clearly, what its origin and meaning are ? It will require fome quicknefs of apprehenfion to make it out in any given time whatever. But you are not the firft who has made things, dark of themfelves, a little darker by endeavouring to explain them.

LEST, ufed as a conjunction, and attended by THAT, means, as you imagine, neither more nor lefs than *That being difmiffed or difcharged, or laid afide.* To give your explanation all the chance poffible, let us not ftand upon trifles ; let us choofe out of thefe three expreffions that which is moft favourable to it, namely, *laid afide :* by ufing it inftead of *I d?,* in the above-mentioned paffage, the whole will run as follows, *You make ufe of thefe arts,* LAID ASIDE THAT, *men might hear reafon from me.* Now, though this conveyance for thought does not run quite fo faft as Englifh conveyances do in general, yet, as it may very well be compared to a dray-cart, dragged on an heavy, flabby, flat-footed horfe, we will not deny it here the appellation of a conveyance for thought ; we fhall only take notice of the direction in which it moves.

I imagine, that when a man fays, *You make ufe of*

thefe

these arts, left men might hear reason from me, their expreſſion implies an apprehenſion in him that ſome thing may happen, and at the ſame time a ſtrong deſire to prevent it. And I am the more inclined to think ſo, as the French uſe upon this occaſion, *De peur que, De crainte que*; the Dutch, *Uyt vreeze dat*; and the Latins their emphatical NE *: expreſſions which all indicate clearly, that the above-mentioned circumſtances do actually take place upon this occaſion. But how can they be implied in this lame and inſipid phraſe, *You make uſe of theſe arts, laid aſide that, men might hear reaſon from me?* It barely declares that ſuch a thing may happen, and has no kind of tendency to expreſs a fear that it may happen, or a deſire to prevent it: LEST THAT, conſequently, muſt convey ſomething more than the bare idea of *quo* or *hoc dimiſſo*: and your ſledge, though we might put up with the ſlowneſs of its motion, yet, as it moves in a contrary direction to that which is intended, muſt be laid aſide in the preſent inſtance.

Dr. Johnſon gives us, in his dictionary, the following deduction of the word LEST.

LEST, *conjunction from the adjective* LEAST, *that not.* On this deduction of the Doctor you make the following remark: *This is a curious one indeed, and it would puzzle as ſagacious a reaſoner as Dr. Johnſon himſelf, to ſupply the middle ſtep to his concluſion, from*

---

* They ſay, indeed, *Cave putes, Cave credas*; but it is evident that NE is underſtood, and that even in this way of ſpeaking there is an ellipſis of *Ut*; and that the phraſe at full length is *Cave ut ne credas*; ſo Terence, *Ulciſcar ut ne impune in nos illuſeris*; and Tully, *Opera datur ut judicia ne fiant*.

LEAST *(which always, however, means something)* to, THAT NOT, which means NONE AT ALL. I beg leave to make some remarks in my turn.

1. If there be any thing curious in the present case, it is your criticism on Dr. Johnson's explanation, and your recommendation of *hoc dimisso,* or *quo dimisso,* in the room of it. From what has been already alledged against it, there is no great hope of *hoc dimisso,* or *quo dimisso,* ever making its way so as to get the start of any explanation whatever ; let us, however, compare them together, by trying their respective efficacy on the above-mentioned passage.

Dr. Johnson's explanation of it is, *You make use of these arts,* THAT *men may* NOT *hear reason from me.*

Your improvement upon Dr. Johnson is, *You make use of these arts.* Why ? *the reason follows : Lezed that,* i. e. *Hoc dimisso—men may hear reason from me.*

Is it not astonishing that a man should plume himself on having substituted this strained and far-fetched manner of speaking, for the easy and natural explanation which precedes ? But say you,

2. LEAST always means something, and Johnson employs it as a mere negative. Quirks and quibbles, Sir, will not do in the search after truth. When I hear it affirmed of a man, that he has friends no where, and least of all at court, I should be glad to know how many friends I may reasonably suppose that man to have at court. Or, when I read in Latin, *Minime gentium, res minime mira, spectaculum mi-*

nime

nime gratum ; or thus, *Operam das ut minime meis ob-
temperent confiliis homines ;* I fhould take it very kindly,
if you would let me know what that fomething is
which the word MINIME implies ; becaufe, when that
is done, it will be an eafy matter, not only to fettle
your difpute with Mr. Harris, about the manner of
fupplying the article in the Greek *, but, moreover,
to adjuft public matters fo, as that there fhall be no
more difcontented people, no more effufion of blood,
and difmemberment of the empire.

3. LEST, in the fenfe of THAT NOT, or the NE em-
phaticum of the Latin, is generally written in the
ancient language thus, LÆST ; and what is more to
the purpofe, it is there preceded by the article THE
or THY. ƿapnoƷe he hine ð læꞃ hi on hƿyle ꞇo
him ineꞇðan. " Caverat ne in aliquam domum ad
" fe introirent †." þæꞇ hẏ ð ꞅolcꞃiht aꞃehꞇon þy
læꞃ æniᴣ man cꞃeðe. That they common right
fhould declare ‡ Ð læꞃ ꝥe ꞅꞃelꞇon, Ne moriamur §.—
And as læꞃ is ufed alfo in the Anglo-Saxon for the
comparative of lyꞇel, parvus, it is evident that ꝥ læꞃ
anfwers to the modern THE, or THAT LESS. ꝥ læꞃꞇ
to THAT LEAST, fupple, OF ALL THINGS; and if fo,
it will require no great effort of genius to find out
the middle ftep from LEST to THAT NOT ; and you
will do well to look for it yourfelf, as it will furnifh
you with an eafy and natural explanation of the word

---

* See Diverfions of Purley, p. 100.

† Bed. Hift. Ecclef. Lib. I. cap. 21.

‡ Alfred's Will, p. 12.

§ Exod. xx. 19.

LEST,

LEST, and put you, perhaps, upon acknowledging, as I think you ought to do, that, in this, as well as in many other inftances, you have been too precipitate in condemning Johnfon.

I have now gone over the greater part of your feventh chapter; and from the remarks I have made, there arifes a ftrong prefumption, that, if a few of your etymologies can bear examination, moft of them cannot; being grounded on words, either not in the language, or not connected with thofe of which they are fuppofed to be the origin. And having proceeded thus far, it will perhaps be expected that I fhould go on, and extend my remarks to the remaining part of your work; but the exceptionable places being lefs numerous there than in the preceding chapters, and moftly of the kind already noticed; fo that in animadverting on them at large, it would hardly be poffible to avoid repetitions; I fhall content myfelf with a few general obfervations, and then conclude.

Notwithftanding the unfavourable impreffions I received from your manner of tracing the conjunctions to their origin, that is, to the primitive word in the language from which they fpring; I muft do you the juftice to fay, that I have read with pleafure, and even with fome advantage, your ninth and tenth chapters, which treat of prepofitions and adverbs. The light in which you place thefe parts of fpeech is new, and well calculated to turn the attention of the ftudious in general from idle and endlefs fubtleties,

to

to the contemplation of truth, and acquisition of real
knowledge. Your deductions here are, upon the
whole, the reverse of what they were before; for,
except such as rest upon supposed imperatives, they
are in general plausible, and many of them unex-
ceptionable. In short, I think this the best part of
the work. I am more particularly pleased with the
following reflexion *: *The explanation and etymology
of these words require a degree of knowledge in all the
ancient languages, and a degree of skill in the application of that knowledge, which I am very far from af-
suming.* After a sentence so full of modesty and dif-
cretion, so much to your honour, one is grieved to
see you meddle with the *benedenste lip, en enderste lip,*
and with *Spic-span,* and *Spik-spelder.* O fie upon
Spic-span and *Spik-spelder* †.

As you seem to aim at some signal distinction in
the etymological career, let me prevail upon you not
to be too free with the Dutch. I know that any one

* P. 491.

† In Dutch they say, *Spik-spelder niew,* and *Spyker,* means a
warehouse, or a magazine; *Spil,* or *Spel,* means a spindle; *Schiet,
Spoel,* the weaver's shuttle; and *Spoelder,* the shuttle thrower. In
Dutch, therefore, *Spik spelder niew* means new from the warehouse,
or the loom, Div. of Parl. p. 508.

N. B. 1. Two points over a single vowel not in use with regard
to Dutch words. 2. *Spyker* means here a nail. 3. *Spel* for Spil,
not in the Dutch language. 4. *Spoelder,* ditto. 5. *Spelder,* here
an oblique case of *Spelde,* a pin ‡. 6. *Spoelder,* in the premisses, a
shuttle-thrower; in the conclusion, a loom. Sum total of the faults
in this article, Six.

‡ See Halma, in Spelde.

is at liberty to mangle and torture it ; but there are a thousand reasons why you should not. For, not to mention that a man may be possessed of an uncommon share of merit, both as a scholar and a gentleman, without knowing a word of it ; this, like other languages, has its true and false currency ; and though the mistaking and tendering the one for the other is deemed but a slight offence in some ; with regard to dealers in etymologies, it is reckoned a capital one. And as the field of glory lies open to you in so many places, why should you attempt to enter it at one so dangerous?

Let me add another piece of advice, which you seem to be much in want of : when you are about some new discovery, take care not to dwell too long upon one and the same thing. It is well known, that by the continual pressure of the same idea upon the mind, its operations are greatly impeded. I remember to have read somewhere of a Greek professor, who, having made it out, as he thought, that the Greek language is the source of all the rest ; at every word he met with, whether in the German or French, Latin or Hebrew, would call out Vox Græca ! and be as positive about it, in case of any demur, as brother Peter about his brown loaf. Though this case is by no means similiar to yours, it puts one neverthelefs in mind of your imperatives.

If you must put our gravity to the proof, by telling us that, *Man join nofe* * ; *Afs be out crupper* ; *figs*

* P. 348.

beginning

beginning Turkey, and the like, are the true prototypes
of a man with a nose ; an afs without a crupper ; figs
from Turkey *, &c. Well and good. We are ready
to pay you the attention which is your due as a man
of learning and genius. But be not too positive ;
and remember, that if, in delivering these sentiments,
we perceive the least attempt, or even desire, to pass
them upon us as articles of faith, we shall think
ourselves at liberty to relax in our attention, and
turn into a jest what cannot be converted to any
other use.

You make WITH, preposition as it is called, the
imperative of WITHAN, Ύιφλν †, *to join*. There is
such a verb in the ancient language, and from its
signification, *conjugare, copulare*, it seems to bear some
affinity to the verb WED in English, and peƀıan in
the Anglo-Saxon. And thus far circumstances seem
to favour your derivation of WITH from WITHAN, *to*
join ; but others strongly militate against it. 1. It is
hardly possible to determine which is the root, sup-
posing there is a real affinity betwixt WITH and
WITHAN. 2. WITH often occurs in a sense which
does by no means accord with *conjugare* & *copulare* ;
as for instance, in the English, to WITHHOLD ; the
Dutch, *weederspreeken* ; the German, *widerstehen* ;
and in many other words, it has the signification
of the Latin particles CORAM, or ITERUM. But
the most ugly circumstance of all, in the present case,

* P. 185. p. 375.   † P. 376.

is

is your having fomewhere elfe derived * the prepofition WITH from the *foi-difant* Anglo-Saxon ᵖᵞᵱᵭᵾ-
ᵵan. I very much fear that this will bring to the
ground your conjecture about WITH from *withan*, to
join, and that *man join nofe* muft be given up as a
loft caufe; unlefs indeed you can prove, as you attempt to do, that there is a fallacy in that prepofition
which few people are aware of; that, Proteus-like,
it is fometimes one thing, and fometimes another;
that in the following phrafes, WITH *mifchance*, WITH
mifadventure, it means *be*, and is the imperative of
ᵖᵞᵱᵬon; whereas in thefe, WITH *evil prefe*, WITH
harde grace, it means JOIN, and comes from WITHAN,
to join †. But this is a hard tafk indeed!

Truth, as you fay, has been improperly imagined
at the bottom of a well: it lies much nearer the fur-
face. Had Mr. Harris and others, inftead of diving
deeper than they had occafion, into Ariftotelian myf-
teries, contented themfelves with obferving plain
facts; they would foon have perceived, that prepofitions and conjunctions were nothing more than nouns
and verbs in difguife; and the chapter of the diftribution and divifion of language would have been fet-
tled and compleat long ago, to the contentment and
joy of every body; whereas, in the way they pro-

---

* Mr. Tyrwhitt has obferved truly, that BY and WITH are often
fynonymous; they are always fo when WITH is the imperative of
ᵱᵞᵱᵬan . . . . . . But Mr. Tyrwhitt is miftaken when he fuppofes
WITH *evil prefe*, WITH *hard grace*, WITH *fory grace*—to have the
fame meaning: for, in thofe three inftances, WITH is the imperative of ᵞIᵠᴧN. Div. of Purl. p. 349. in a note.

† P. 349.

ceeded,

ceeded, their labour was immenfe, and the benefit equal to nothing.

Happy thofe, who, in their endeavours to explain fcience, are allowed to look behind the veil which conceals her from the common eye. Whatever be the object of their purfuit, if they are but allowed to contemplate it in its true light, and give fuch information about it as has not been given yet; they think themfelves fufficiently rewarded, and perfevere with joy in application.

To many the ftudy of particles may feem unpleafant and unprofitable; but it is neither. The happinefs which is felt by the Philofopher, and that enjoyed by the Grammarian, are nearly on a par, provided both originate in the difcovery of truth. As to the utility of it, though trifling in itfelf, it leads to things of the utmoft confequence; and the moft dignified of all fciences, Theology, often deigns to confult her humble hand-maid, the fcience of particles, the better to fteer her way through the many difficulties which furround her *.

Profeffor Schultens was the firft philologift who fufpected prepofitions, conjunctions, particles in general to be no more than nouns or verbs, and refufed therefore to make feparate claffes of them, among thofe that comprehend the parts of fpeech.

* Ac ne ipfa quidem, opinor omnium difciplinarum regina, theologia ducet indignum admoveri fibi manus ac debitum exhiberi officium a pedifequa grammatica: quæ tametfi nonnullis eft pofterior dignitate, nullius certe opera magis neceffaria. In minimis verfatur, fed fine quibus nemo evafit maximus. Nugas agit, fed quæ ad feria ducunt. Erafmus Epift. Lib. IV. Ep. 7.

But

But he confined himſelf in the application of this truth to the learned languages. You are the firſt who applied it to thoſe which are called modern. It would be wrong not to acknowledge, that in this you have rendered the literary world an important ſervice. For though you have not been allowed to proceed far in this career without frequent miſtakes, yet your progreſs through it has been ſufficiently marked with ſucceſs to put others upon making ſome further diſcoveries. That this may be the final reſult of your lucubrations, and that you may live to ſee your ſyſtem receive all the improvements of which it is ſuſceptible, is the ſincere wiſh of

Your moſt obedient ſervant,

I. CASSANDER.

www.ingramcontent.com/pod-product-compliance
Lightning Source LLC
Chambersburg PA
CBHW020308090426
42735CB00009B/1262